The Elements of Foucault

posthumanities

CARY WOLFE, SERIES EDITOR

(continued on page 144)

THE ELEMENTS
OF FOUCAULT

GREGG LAMBERT

posthumanities 55

University of Minnesota Press

Minneapolis

London

Published by the University of Minnesota Press
111 Third Avenue South, Suite 290
Minneapolis, MN 55401-2520
http://www.upress.umn.edu

ISBN 978-1-5179-0877-5 (hc)
ISBN 978-1-5179-0878-2 (pb)

A Cataloging-in-Publication record for this book is available from the Library of Congress.

Printed in the United States of America on acid-free paper

The University of Minnesota is an equal-opportunity educator and employer.

UMP BmB 2020

Contents

Article I
On "Foucault"

I repeat: there is not, behind the face, a secret self governing
our acts or receiving our impressions; we are only the series of
those imaginary acts and those errant impressions.

—Jorge Luis Borges, *A New Refutation of Time*

Why write another book on Foucault? Why now? And for whom? These
are questions that have preoccupied me recently, but especially when I
was close to finishing this book and the last question started ringing again
in my ears. Of course, this ringing was accompanied by the other voices:
"Isn't there too much commentary already?" "What possible difference
will one more commentary make?" "Hasn't everything already been said?
Especially about *this* author?" Of course, in some ways, I completely agree.
Moreover, I recall that Foucault also confessed, in the beginning of his inaugural lecture at the Collège de France concerning the future of his own
project, to hearing voices, which he resolved by citing the following line
from Beckett's *Molloy*: "You must go on. I can't go on. I'll go on."[1]

So, *I'll go on too*!

Today, the numerous existing commentaries on "Foucault" are like
tiny grains of sand that have accumulated into massive dunes in a vast
desert. I suppose, according to this image (please excuse the lack of pro-
fundity), every commentator actually believes that her tiny grain of sand
will be precisely the exact weight that will cause the huge pile to topple
over. In fact, this is often not the case, and the little tiny grain of sand is

simply added to the pile, causing it to grow higher. Eventually this leads to a kind of unhappy consciousness that covers the entire genre of commentary with a thick and heavy atmosphere. Foucault himself describes this as the moment "when all things come eventually to take the form of discourse, when everything may be said and when anything becomes an excuse for pronouncing a discourse, it will be because all things having manifested and exchanged meanings, and will then all be able to return to the silent inferiority of self-consciousness."[2]

The actual function of commentary, therefore, is to disguise or displace the unhappy circular and interior movement of self-consciousness in the relation between the primary and secondary texts.[3] This creates a movement of verticality and the pyramidal form of discourse, which in reality is simply a flat, two-dimensional space. It produces the top heaviness of the original text and, beneath it, the quasi-anonymous murmuring of the discourse that speaks from an unfathomable depth of what remains unsaid, and yet to be said. However, as Foucault points out, this deep infinity is a false appearance and only serves to disguise the repetition that the commentary performs by disguising the reappearance of the original enunciation under a sign of difference. Borges's description of the version of Don Quixote under the name of Pierre Menard—we should remember, actually an exact reproduction of the original—is merely a supreme example of this fiction, since the phrase "truth, whose mother is history" is purported to mean something completely different in each version, and the original statement no longer produces a division between the text and its copy. From this point onward, Foucault writes, "the novelty lies no longer in what is said, but in its reappearance."[4]

This dilemma is only exacerbated by the "awesome materiality" of discourse itself, for which Foucault provides the corresponding image of the archeological strata. According to this archeological image of thought, the history of commentary does not comprise a single duration of time but rather forms a kind of broken and discontinuous piling of strata, or multiplicity of durations, all of which are designated by the same proper name, which now functions as a common noun and sometimes as an adjective (e.g., "Foucault").[5] At this moment, precisely, we witness the birth of the "author-function," which is originally revealed as the operator of the open multiplicity of a ponderous and nearly infinite volume of commentary—

although its real function is to control, constrain, or restrict the circulation of discourse precisely by transforming, in special circumstances, the proper name into a signifier and the text into an object of knowledge and discipline.

Of course, as a rule, Foucault always tends to emphasize the negativity that lurks beneath the sheer positivity of the orders of commentary and discipline to make visible their constraining and rarifying forces. For example, he writes:

> We tend to see, in an author's fertility, in the multiplicity of commentaries and in the development of a discipline so many infinite resources available for the creation of new discourse. Perhaps so, but they are nonetheless principles of constraint, and it is probably impossible to appreciate their positive, multiplicative role without first taking into consideration their restrictive, constraining role.[6]

Therefore, along with the rule of commentary and the identity of an author-function, "discipline" is a second order for what Foucault names the "subjection of discourse."

Foucault's specific definition of the term of subjection is meant in both positive and negative senses, that is, as the creation of subjectivity as well as its limitation or constraint—on one hand, the protection of discourse from both internal errors that would threaten its unity, and on the other, a protection from the external dangers of chance elements and misappropriations. For while the function of commentary "limited the hazards of discourse through the action of an identity taking the form of repetition and sameness," and the author-function limits the same chance element through a procedure that resembles "subjective interpellation" (Althusser), disciplines are defined as concrete assemblages of objects and methods and by a selected number of propositions that are taken to be true. In other words, these propositions will serve as axioms as in geometry or logic, since their primary role is to fix the limits of discourse by effecting a "permanent reactivation of the rules" for the inclusion and exclusion of new propositions, objects, and methods.[7] Rather than liberating the text, therefore, the primary function of discipline is to subject it to a discursive order. "Discourse thus nullifies itself, in reality, by placing itself at the disposal of the signifier."[8] From this point onward, Foucault observes, disciplines constitute a system of control in the production of discourse.

Since the 1969 inaugural lecture "L'Ordre du discours," and the accompanying paper, "What Is an Author?," what Foucault originally called the "author-function" has undergone a number of significant transformations. Nevertheless, today the order of disciplines still constitutes a powerful system of control in the production of discourse by imposing limits on the possible forms of individuality and the "I," especially since subjects still "must fulfill some onerous and complex conditions before they can be admitted within a given discipline."[9] As Foucault had already foreseen in the concluding pages of *The Order of Things* concerning the transformation of the human sciences, the recent decline of the "author-function" in certain disciplines, such as philosophy and literary criticism, only constitutes the effect and constellation of the rise of disciplinary authority of the social sciences.[10] This observation is certainly not global, and even in the social sciences, a certain disciplinary division still exists around the question of method, whether quantitative and statistical, theoretical or speculative. Nevertheless, what is most important to notice is that many of the disciplines that formerly enlisted the author-function have instituted in its place a series of transdiscursive objects (e.g., race, sexuality, politics, matter, life) that now assumes a similar function in the institution of knowledge, even though these objects cannot be ascribed by any particular discipline that would produce them as objects of knowledge and discourse. Unlike in the order of commentary, moreover, what is presupposed as the point of departure for analysis in this new disciplinary context is not some original meaning of the text that must be rediscovered, nor an image of thought that must be resuscitated from the history of error, but instead the creation of a new discursive framework for the construction of new statements, since "in order for discipline to exist, there must be the possibility of formulating—and of doing so *ad infinitum*—*fresh propositions*" (i.e., new axioms).[11]

With the foregoing observations, I believe I have discovered a response to my guiding questions: "Isn't there too much commentary already?" "What possible difference will one more commentary possibly make?" "Hasn't everything already been said?" The simple answer to the last question is "Of course not!" If the overriding demand of the new form of discipline is a constant production of fresh propositions in accordance with the rules of inclusion and exclusion (i.e., discursive polemics), then the history of previous statements must also be grouped accordingly, producing the archeological image of discontinuity between the different strata and creating the different arrangements of objects and statements within each discursive grouping.

It is not merely accidental that the preceding observation can also be applied to the genealogy of Foucault's own author-function in the period following the 1970s up to the present moment. Especially with the recent appearance of the lectures from the Collège de France, there has been a significant shift and disorienting effect cast upon the earlier discursive groupings of Foucault's project, which were primarily based on the published writings that preceded his death in 1984. For English-speaking readers, this genealogy has only been compounded by the history of the translation of his major publications and interviews into English, which has created what I will call the "four ages of 'Foucault'": first, the age of *The Order of Things* (1970) and *The Archeology of Knowledge* (1972), concerning discursive practices and the history of representation; second, the age of *Discipline and Punish* (1977), concerning the micro-organization of power; third, the age of *The History of Sexuality, Vol. 1* (1978), concerning the "repressive hypothesis" and "the *dispositif* of sexuality"; and finally, fourth, the age biopolitics, the new perspective on power that appears in the lecture courses, beginning with the publication of *"Society Must Be Defended"* (2003) and, more recently, *The Birth of Biopolitics* (2008).[12]

According to the archeological image of discontinuity in the passage from one discursive grouping to the next, in each and every age, we will also find a dominant "anti-Foucault" that is defined by the discursive polemics surrounding each "Foucault"—that is, "Foucault, the Structuralist," "Foucault, the Eurocentric and 'neo-colonial' theorist," "Foucault, the misogynist and moral hedonist," and finally, for our current age, "Foucault, the Neo-Liberal." For each age a different "Foucault," and an "Anti-Foucault" for every age.

It is clear from the secondary criticism and commentaries that have emerged within each separate age that there is almost no overlapping of the archeological strata, nor even the memory of the major themes and discursive polemics in passing from one strata to the next, echoing a major, but forgotten, axiom that belonged to the first age of "Foucault": the radical "rupture" between different epochs of representation in the history of the "will to knowledge." For example, in taking up the most recent example of this transformation of the "author-function," the disciplinary demand for "fresh propositions" can be vividly demonstrated by the fact that many of his editors and closest readers chose simply to disregard the author's own wishes *not to publish* the transcripts of the lecture courses. As Stuart Elden summarizes this history: "The 'no posthumous publications' injunction was once followed faithfully; then interpreted generously; and is now almost completely disregarded."[13] In some ways, this perfectly illustrates the relation between writing and death that was a frequent theme in the first age, when Foucault also observed a strange reversal in contemporary relationship between writing and the author: "Whereas previously a work had the duty of creating immortality, it now attains the right to kill, to become the murderer of its author."[14] Accordingly, the fate of Foucault's final will is not unrelated to the similar fate of Kafka in the sense that both cases vividly demonstrate the demand of the great oeuvre to sacrifice the subject of the author.

Of course, some readers might immediately object that it would be ridiculous to argue that Foucault was not in some ways an "author" of the discourse of the lectures. Nevertheless, the inclusion of the lectures has reopened some critical questions concerning the historical mutability of any author-function, which never belongs to a stable system of references. (As Foucault himself argued, "the 'author-function' is not universal or constant in all discourse.")[15] Concerning this most recent transformation, therefore, we might excavate the following questions from the first age of "Foucault," which appear at the end of "What Is an Author?":

> "What are the modes of existence of this discourse?" "Where does it come from; how is it circulated; who controls it?" "What placements are determined for possible subjects?" "Who can fulfill these diverse functions of the subject?" [of "Foucault"] And finally: "What matter who's speaking?"[16]

In the current age of "Foucault," moreover, very few would consider returning to an earlier "Foucault," much less the "Structuralist Foucault," to whip up a fresh batch of propositions for interpreting the author-function of the lectures. Why is this so? It is so because in part, these questions belong to a previous stratum, that is, prior to the period of *Discipline and Punish* and *The History of Sexuality* (circa 1975), which is traditionally viewed as the departure from the earlier discursive grouping of statements and works and the commencement of the analytic of *pouvoir du jour*. Second, as I have already intimated, this prehistory has already been understood to be dominated by a perceived structuralist methodology, which has since been judged (even by some of his closest and most faithful readers) as an error that Foucault himself had to correct after a first period of silence between 1969 and 1975.

In his own genealogical study, Jeffrey Nealon summarizes the dominant disciplinary narrative as follows:

> Foucault's early "structuralist" work fails to provide the critical wedge he's seeking, so he abandons it—after 1969's *Archaeology of Knowledge*—to take up the study of power in the 1970s, in the wake of the upheavals of May 1968. However, the two most famous "power books," 1975's *Discipline and Punish* and 1976's first volume of *The History of Sexuality*, likewise comprise a failed project (though for very different reasons than the early structuralist project: archaeology fails to account for the bridges among words and things, while the genealogical work on power is—one might say—seen as having been too successful, too totalizing and demoralizing). Insofar as Foucault so convincingly demonstrates that power is indeed everywhere, capillary and molecular, how can we possibly resist it? How can we be anything but dupes for power? Hoping finally to answer this nagging question of resistance, Foucault turns in his late work to the ethical project of making one's life a work of art.[17]

Nealon argues against what he rightly discerns as basically a bildungsroman narrative that has dominated the traditional studies of Foucault. Rather than seeing his post-1969 shifts of emphasis as a series of failures or dialectical sublations, the shifts of emphasis are more productively understood as a series of "intensifications" that might assist us in thinking about (if not actually "resisting") the real mutations and intensifications of power that we've seen since Foucault's death in 1984.[18]

As another well-known example, in 1986, Gilles Deleuze published an important study of Foucault's entire philosophy, in which he actually did offer a series of fresh propositions concerning this same bildungsroman. However, the explanation Deleuze offered for the supposed second lapse of silence between the first and second volumes of *The History of Sexuality*—of course, it would never occur to him to view the lectures as part of the work—is more interesting than the traditional narrative because it posits a moment of crisis rather than failure. Deleuze asks:

> What happened during the fairly long silence following *The History of Sexuality*? Perhaps Foucault felt slightly uneasy about the book: had he not trapped himself within the concept of power relations? . . . If at the end of it Foucault finds himself in an impasse, this is not because of his conception of power but rather because he found the impasse to be where power itself places us, in both our lives and our thoughts, as we run up against it in our smallest truths. . . . Foucault felt it necessary to carry out a general reshuffle in order to unravel this path which was so tangled up in the others that it remained hidden: it is this re-centering which Foucault puts forward in the general introduction to *The Use of Pleasure*.[19]

Deleuze's stylistic "portrait" marks a departure from most of the secondary criticism hailing from U.S. and U.K. scholars in Nealon's account, since he claims that *Foucault did not fail; actually, power did!* In other words, if we cannot resist, according to the earlier image of power relations provided in the works of the middle period, it is not the fault of the theory but rather the way that a certain determination of power has come to saturate everything, leaving us no exterior point from which to resist.[20]

I believe we have now arrived at the current age of "Foucault," if only because many of the issues addressed in the preceding discussion now seem quite distant, and most have been forgotten by contemporary readers. The strata have been reshuffled many times, and there are new discursive groupings and a number of fresh propositions around the concepts of "biopower" and "biopolitics." Most of all, the reason why the narrative problem of Foucault's so-called period of silence has been forgotten (whether this was understood tragically, heroically, or merely as a symptom of malaise and personal failure) is simply because, in 1997, the lectures began to appear to perfectly fill in the gap in the discourse between 1975 and 1984. Not only was it revealed that Foucault was speaking all along—in fact, he was speaking incessantly (a bit like Beckett's character in *The Unnamable*, a mouth speaking inside a barrel)!—the problem today is to get him to shut up, to stop talking, even though the volume of discourse continues to grow to pandemic proportions. If the discourse around the lecture courses eclipsed so many of the critical and epistemological problems raised in the first three ages (e.g., "the repressive hypothesis"), today it is because the lectures have offered so much rich material for producing new statements and new transdiscursive objects at the intersection of knowledge and power. Consequently, any return to the "early Foucault" would seem like a regression to earlier propositions that serve no use for the discipline of "Foucault studies" today.

The method I employ for entering into this troubled history is not to effect a "return to Foucault" according to the traditional genre of philosophical hermeneutics, which seeks to recover an original conceptual personage, or to "reinitiate" an image of thought through its various gaps, points of blindness, incomprehension, omission, and silence. (As Foucault cautioned many times, this only represents a certain historical institution of the "will to truth" that belongs to a disciplinary order of philosophy.) In fact, recalling the voices I heard at the beginning, it has only recently occurred to me that the very gesture of a "return to Foucault" would have absolutely no effect in rectifying the discursive polemics that surround Foucault's thought today, nor would any simple recitation of Foucault's original propositions on power change anyone's mind. And yet, perhaps this only confirms that the function of the author has indeed changed and that today what Foucault calls the "transformation of discursive practice" is not effected by any "return to the author" but rather by certain global statements and propositions that take as their object an entire system of thought, either to uphold it or reject it altogether. At this point, I realized that to engage in this already highly polemicized field of discourse, I needed to find a new set of weapons, which I happened to find in Descartes's *more geometrico*. It is a bit like the statement by Rose, one of Kafka's characters in "The Country Doctor": "You never know what you're going to find in your own basement."[21]

In response to this new situation, therefore, we might ask what has changed and what function discursive polemics serve in the contemporary institution of the "will to truth." Here I will risk reactivating an earlier set of questions for examining the contemporary constellation of truth, knowledge, and power: What are the modes of existence of the discourse on "Foucault"? How does this discourse circulate? What placements are determined for its subjects? Who is qualified to fulfill these functions today? In other words, "Who is speaking?" Moreover, I wonder whether this last question must be heard from a completely different understanding of the subject of discourse today. In *L'Ordre du discours*, Foucault first addressed the polemical opposition between true and false statements as "a third order of inclusion and exclusion" that is supported by a system of institutions imposing and manipulating this division, neither without constraint, "nor without an element, at least, of violence."[22] It is according to this third order he says that, historically, the "will to truth" has become a system of inclusion and exclusion that materially relies on a complex array of mechanisms, rules, authorities, disciplines, academic societies, publishing systems, universities, and so on. (In fact, it is this third order of inclusion and exclusion that determines the concept of dispositif six years later in the first volume of *The History of Sexuality*.) In the earlier lecture, following the work of Canguilhem on the history of the natural sciences, he also observed that even before a given statement can be judged as either true or false, the subject must already be "within the true" *(dans le vrai)*. This requirement assumes a blatantly tautological form that the disciplinary order could only resolve by instituting as a condition of the subject of knowledge a kind of blackmail: one can only *be in the true* if, even before speaking, only if one already belonged to the order of discipline, and this obeyed the rules of its own discursive polity. According to Foucault, it is within this implicit form of blackmail *(le chantage)* that one of the most important functions of disciplinary order was to ensure that these rules are reactivated every time one begins to speak.[23] Of course, he returns to this form of blackmail again in a late essay around the question of the Enlightenment.[24]

If we observe this function today, however, within the context of what I would call a postdisciplinary order of discourse, first we must simply acknowledge that our contemporary situation bears very little resemblance to the institutions and academic disciplines that Foucault addressed in 1969 before an audience of mostly French academics, or to the situation Foucault addressed before his death in 1984. Of course, I do not mean to say that there are no longer any disciplines but only that in certain areas of theoretical inquiry, the dangerous division between true and false knowledge is no longer operated by the historical disciplines themselves, for the most part, but has been replaced by what I defined earlier as global polemics over a finite number of transdiscursive objects.[25] Moreover, it is clear today that the demand for fresh propositions does not primarily issue from any disciplinary order of knowledge but rather from what Foucault describes in the lectures as an "imperative theoretical discourse" that alternatively goes by the names of "politics" and "the political."[26]

Therefore, in addition to the author-function that constrains the awesome materiality of discourse by individuating the form of enunciation, and disciplines constituting a relative system of control in the production and reproduction of discourse, we might hypothesize that today the third order of inclusion and exclusion operates not only upon statements that are determined as true or false according to a disciplinary order but directly on bodies, identities, and subjectivities. In other words, *and in some ways completely reversing Foucault's previous formulation,* today the question "What matter who's speaking?" has become more important than ever before, even though this question often appears strangely decided even before the act of speaking itself. Here we must ask: What is the nature of this subject's authority? How does it appear? Why has it become so effective in controlling the circulation of discourse and knowledge, especially in those regions of knowledge that we sometimes too hastily call "the political"? In fact, could the statement that Foucault made concerning what he called the "austere monarchy of sexuality" be applied to what we might today call the "austere monarchy of the political": that "the irony of this dispositif is in having us believe that our 'liberation' is in the balance"?[27]

Of course, some readers might rightfully object that this is certainly nothing new, since this third order has always functioned to include only certain subjects "within the true" and has been proven historically to exclude many more subjects than it has included. The fact that today this order of inclusion and exclusion appears to operate more out in the open so that the question "what matter who's speaking?" is more visible to everyone is at least an improvement over the previous orders of discourse that operated from a more or less hidden vantage point depending on where one was situated in the social field. And yet, to recall Deleuze's earlier observation, the problem of power today is that it has permeated every perspective to a point of saturating the entire social field, so that there is no external space for the objectivization of these power relations within a form of knowledge or discipline. In some important respects, this challenges the preceding claim to a greater degree of visibility, since the perspective from which power appears is bound to a hidden point of view concerning the subjectivation of power itself, which is why the appearance of power has become a polemical concept sine qua non.

Perhaps what Canguilhem said of the concept of "life" can also be applied to the transdisciplinary and transdiscursive object of power: it is impure, in the Kantian sense, which is the same as calling it a metaphysical concept because its meaning is informed by too many disciplines.[28] Thus we can only speak of a multiplicity of conceptualizations (mechanical, biological, physicochemical, thermodynamic, philosophical or ontological, and, lastly, theological). In other words, it is this multiplicity of significations of power that is the true cause of its polemical definition as a complex idea that emerges within the modern dispositif of biopolitics. Today, moreover, is it by chance that the arguments concerning the existence of power (concerning its nature, form, and disposition) seem to have taken the same form of polemical dispute as the arguments over the existence of God in the seventeenth century? My question would be whether this is a coincidence, or could we say it is because power today has assumed the position of a metaphysical principle, formerly occupied by the polemical disputes over the existence of God?

Therefore I will conclude this preliminary article by explaining, according to the foregoing hypothesis, my reasons for resorting to what is basically a seventeenth-century method of presentation in this study of Foucault's analytic of biopower. First, we should recall that Descartes first applied this method of presentation precisely as a weapon to engage in a highly polemicized field of opinion and belief over metaphysical principles, which I will apply to the current polemical field of ideas concerning power, and particularly to the polemics that surround the concept of biopower that Foucault first proposed in 1975. Second, this association is based on my discernment of Foucault's own use of this manner of presenting his analysis of biopower, in terms of what he called "postulates and problems," beginning in the first volume of *The History of Sexuality* and then in the first session of every lecture course between 1975 and 1979.[29] In other words, Foucault himself resorts to this method to engage with the theoretical and analytical discourse that was permeated by the imperative discourse of politics in his own context, if only as a manner of producing the necessary theoretical distance for reflection and knowledge of power relations. Thus, as one of the methods of abstraction that belongs to the philosophical arsenal (mathematics and logic being others), it is important to see the *more geometrico* as the creation of a purely artificial space for reflecting on the real relations that have become habitual and ingrained throughout the history of the representations of power.

If I wanted to exaggerate my use of this method, in the manner of Borges, I would simply describe my study as a seventeenth-century reply to a twenty-first-century debate over metaphysical principles. Of course, I realize that this method of presentation has both its advantages and its disadvantages. The disadvantages are that the contemporary reader will be unfamiliar with it, and thus the question of the method itself will need to be clarified in the course of the presentation, which I attempt to do in the first part of the second article on the elements of the analysis of biopower: method, conceptual device, and the grid of intelligibility. (In the third article, I discover a fourth element in the notion of "milieu.") The advantages are that this style will place the reader on unfamiliar terrain, and, I hope, this will suspend some of the most stubborn opinions concerning Foucault's own conceptualizations of power. Consequently, the second article should be regarded as a three-dimensional model of Foucault's major conceptual device (dispositif), which the reader should be able to view from several different perspectives. As for those readers who Descartes himself referred to as the most "stubborn and quarrelsome readers . . . who like to contradict for the sake of contradicting, and who are busy looking for counter-arguments," to save them some time, in place of a formal conclusion, I have simply tacked on a more synthetic presentation of the entire analytic of biopower and work backward by beginning with the common notions of sovereignty and the natural being of power.[30]

Finally, in conclusion, it is important that the contemporary reader understand that the geometrical manner is intended as a peaceful suspension of the usual violence associated with polemics, even though this aspect of violence is thought to be restricted to the affective region of discourse alone. This is why Descartes wrote "meditations" rather than "disputations," which were a favorite vehicle for the philosophers of his time, *just as they continue to be the dominant style of the imperative discourse of truth and politics in our own!* However, the obvious advantage of the former method, which is the reason that I have decided to employ it in my own study of "Foucault," is that it has no way of compelling belief, even for the most argumentative or careless reader, but simply asks that the reader lay down his own weapons and join me in meditating and attending closely on the notion of power within its modern dispositifs.

Article II
On the Elements of Biopower
(circa 1975–1979)

1. Method

After years of reading Foucault, recently I have come to understand the later lectures as providing the basic "elements" (in the Euclidian sense) that can be used for constructing the different figures of power relations. In the Greek, "elements" are to geometrical figures what letters are to language (e.g., a = point, b = line, c = plane or surface). In Euclidian geometry, the function of the postulates (which follow the definition of the elements) is demonstrative rather than didactic. A postulate is not a proposition, as in logic, but rather more like an instruction concerning how to draw a figure using a straightedge or compass (e.g., "1. Let it be postulated to draw a straight line from any point to any point.")[1] The figure itself (or *machina*), sometimes called a "conceptual device" *(un dispositif),* also happens to be the term Foucault specifically chooses to describe his various demonstrations of how power operates through a complex and highly artificial organization of historical institutions and discursive orders as well as new statistical knowledges and concrete techniques.[2]

Anytime one attempts to define the concept of power in Foucault, one must first address the question of his own method. Therefore, in defining the elements of Foucault's analysis of power, it seems fitting to follow his own order of presentation by first posing the question, What is a method? Briefly, a method is defined as a procedure or technique, especially in a logical or systematic way, or, even more generally, a method can simply be defined as any order or system of doing anything whatsoever, because it involves a sequence of actions governed by rules within a definite plan of action. Beginning with Descartes, philosophy borrowed its own understanding of method from mathematics and geometry, in particular, and it is by means of a geometric manner of presentation that one understands oneself to be doing philosophy rather than theology or law. As Leibniz wrote, "the Greeks reasoned with the greatest possible justice in mathematics, and they have left to the human species models of the art of presentation."[3]

In his *Objections*, Descartes divides method into two orders, analytic and synthetic, and reveals the true reason why philosophy must resort to the latter by beginning with the common notions and "disposing the proofs" and by employing a long series of definitions, postulates, axioms, theorems, and problems. This was owed not to any lack of clarity of the basic metaphysical principles (at least, for Descartes) but rather to the innate limitations of the "most stubborn and quarrelsome readers" (basically, other philosophers and theologians) who remain stuck to their sense-based opinions that have become ingrained in them through the years, and who often have the habit of contradicting just for the sake of it.[4] Thus, to recover the original meaning of *more geometrico* from its seventeenth-century context, it was deployed as a weapon of battle in an already polemicized field of opinion concerning first principles (in this case, the principle of God). This strategic situation may help to explain Foucault's ironic allusion to the synthetic geometrical method *(more geometrico dispositae)* in first presenting his arguments concerning the ideas of sexuality and power, as we will see in the synthetic presentation of the "dispositif of sexuality"—before an audience composed of psychoanalysts, the French Left (including official members of the Communist Party), and especially the student remnants of the *soixant-huitard*.

Foucault's most complete statement of method is first given in the fourth part of *The History of Sexuality* and then at the beginning of each of the lecture courses between 1975 and 1979. These excursions on the question of method must be understood precisely as moments when Foucault basically returns to his earlier postulates in order to refine them—and in some cases, to subtract and fundamentally revise the traditional notions of sovereignty and juridical concepts in constructing the new dispositifs of power. Given the history of the critical reception of Foucault's various new dispositifs (such as sexuality, discipline, security, populations, territory, biopower), I will argue that one of the primary reasons his analysis has been the subject of such ongoing controversy is that his method causes a *deformation* of the common notion in which power "must not be sought in the primary existence of a central point, in a unique source of sovereignty from which secondary and descendent forms would emanate," as in a Platonic system of ideas.[5]

To demonstrate what I call Foucault's geometrical manner *(more geometrico)*, I will pay special attention to why Foucault chooses early on to "bypass" the traditional notion of sovereign power and instead to propose what modern geometers would call an "axiomatized theory," according to which any axioms that cannot be proven as necessarily true are subtracted at the very beginning of the analysis, even though they may be deduced in the conclusion. This method is stated quite explicitly in the first volume of *The History of Sexuality* (in the section appropriately titled "Method"): "This analysis, made in terms of power, must not assume that the sovereignty of the state, the form of the law, or the over-all unity of a domination are given at the outset; rather, these are only the terminal forms that power takes."[6]

Given the importance that Foucault places on the question of method throughout his analysis of power, we shouldn't assume that he is merely applying an already established formal or epistemological procedure, since he often declares that he is not simply "doing philosophy." Therefore we must understand that his own manner was not simply applying an already existing philosophical method to a treatment of his subjects (power, discipline, sexuality, liberty, security, biopolitical life) but rather proposing a new set of epistemological rules for first determining the object itself, namely, power—or, more accurately, "power relations," because power is neither a being nor an entity but rather is composed of relations that are external to their terms. In other words, Foucault is clearly a "nominalist" in most epistemological matters (and in the history of philosophy, nominalism has also been called "conceptualism"). Especially concerning the question of what is power, Foucault says, "One needs to be nominalistic, indeed: power is not an institution, and not a structure; neither is it a certain strength we are endowed with; rather, it is the name that one attributes to a complex strategical situation in a particular society."[7]

Foucault's unique approach to the subject of power is a reference to an

Aristotelian understanding of knowledge as *technē*, a term often translated from the Greek as "craft" or "art," that is, the power to intervene into nature *(phusis)* and bend it to another end, causing it to swerve or deviate from its own immanent and naturally self-propagating form. (This is also the essence of the tool, which, as Canguilhem will argue, can also be found in animals and plants.)[8] Moreover, this peculiar capacity also requires a sufficient knowledge of a second power *(potentia)* that is capable of intervening into the first and is coupled to certain practical subjects of knowledge endowed with an effective knowledge of the matter itself, what techniques or tools to employ, and the probable outcomes. Therefore what is peculiar to the "political animal" *(zoon politikon)* is the reproduction of a thoroughly strategic knowledge that is capable of entering into either combat or debate concerning the particular end of a particular intervention, whether we are talking about the carpenter's debate with a piece of wood, the sculptor's debate with a block of marble, the painter's debate with lines and colors, or the politician's debate with the opinions of her citizenry, which are like wood to the carpenter, or lines to the painter.

If we do not first grasp this Aristotelian determination of *technē*, then we will not understand why Foucault will often oppose his own method of analysis to any existing definition of philosophical or scientific epistemology. For Foucault, the epistemological question concerns the specific nature of the knowledge or techniques employed in the exercise of power, that is, the strategic intervention into power relations to shape them into a definite form or to assign a particular goal to the function. As in the case of the Aristotelian understanding of the function, this knowledge does not always take the form of analytic judgment but rather of a practical or synthetic form of judgment. In other words, recall the famous anecdote from Kant's *Critique of Judgment* that also applies this distinction between technique and knowledge: "Camper describes very exactly how the best shoe must be made, but he, doubtless, was not able to turn one out himself." Canguilhem will later conclude from the same anecdote that "every technique essentially and positively includes a vital originality [i.e., efficient causality] irreducible to rationalization."[9] It is this understanding of the invention of new strategies and techniques of power as expressions of "vital originality" that will fundamentally influence Foucault's understanding of the nature of technique and why Foucault later defines this specific knowledge more in terms of the practical subject of art than as a subject of science (for example, as in the phrase the "art of governmentality," which is often employed in the last lectures and interviews).

At the same time, we must ask, would this not condemn the idea of power itself to an essentially positive (i.e., historical) form of irrationality that is gradually ascribed to the Unconscious beginning in the twentieth century by psychoanalysis? This is a problem that Foucault addresses early on in *The Order of Things* (1966) concerning the emergence of psychoanalysis and ethnography as what he calls "bastard-" or "counter-sciences" that will unfound any positivistic idea of the rationality of the human sciences.[10] Beginning in the period of *Discipline and Punish* (1975) and *The History of Sexuality* (1976), however, he will argue that it is a matter not of reducing the knowledge of power to vital instinctual or unconscious forces that resist a general form of scientific rationality but rather of discovering the form of knowledge that is deployed in its techniques and concrete assemblages of power relations. Therefore, if the history of political philosophy can be described (as Foucault often does) as a repeated attempt to rationalize the techniques of power in the idea of a "system," often forgetting or ignoring altogether the unconscious origin of its concrete mechanisms and its historical dispositifs, then Foucault will begin by asking what is the specific nature of the technical knowledge that is deployed by these mechanisms and is responsible for their invention, a knowledge whose subject is practical (a subject of will or desire) and not necessarily theoretical (a subject of Reason).

THE PROBLEM OF "RATIONALIZING POWER"

The question of *technē* also introduces an epistemological problem that Foucault will constantly highlight when he addresses the question of method for deducing a knowledge of power relations: if power originates in a manner that is in some ways "irreducible to rationalization," then how does one go about the business of rationalizing it? It is this simple question that revolves around the problem of method in Foucault, which he repeatedly and cautiously restates at the beginning of every lecture course in the Collège of France, from the mid-1970s onward, concerning a rationale for security, populations, biopolitics, and, neoliberal governmentally. Finally, it is the relationship between techniques of self-government and the government of others that is the focus of the lecture courses after 1978.[11]

What does Foucault mean when he says that power cannot—and, in other cautious moments, *should not!*—be "rationalized"?

First, it means that power relations can no longer be rationalized as a form of natural right, nor according to the model of contract theory, which was always already a speculative fiction at best (or romance, as in the case of Rousseau), because power is not something that can first be possessed and subsequently alienated like a property or commodity. (Spinoza already made this critique of natural right in the *Ethics,* when he said that you can't give up a power to another that you don't first possess as a natural attribute of your own individual substance.)

Second, it means that power is not a natural being but rather artifice, a technique, or a strategy. Power is neither a soul, as in Aristotle; a substance, as in Spinoza; nor a subject, as in Hegel and Marx. Thus, after subtracting the natural and historical attributes of power, once again, we are left with a strictly nominalist definition offered earlier.

A second maxim that Foucault often invokes concerns quantity, which is to say that one must not rationalize too much the existing power relations—even if it is in the name of the "oppressed"! On first glance, this might appear to contradict the aim of his earlier works on madness or discipline, alongside his activist role on behalf of prisoners, but the explanation he gives is repeated again at the beginning of the lecture course of January 11, 1978 (and then again, in January the next year), where he declares that what he is performing under the term of "philosophy" (or, as he calls his own discourse, "a politics of truth") should not be understood in any way as laying down "a general theory of power, nor even the beginning of one," and that its didactic or imperative senses should only be taken as a series of "tactical pointers . . . in the circle of struggle and truth" (i.e., the field of real power relations).[12] In other words, he qualifies the didactic sense of his own "politics of truth" (his "philosophy," by another name) by subtracting any generalized or moral imperative (i.e., "love this, hate that, this is good, this is bad," etc.) but instead seeks to offer some practical research for orienting oneself within a field of real forces. "Of course," as he immediately qualifies the concrete field of his own investigations, "it's up to me, and to those who are working in the same direction, to know on what fields of real forces we need to get our bearings in order to make a tactically effective analysis."[13]

In a little-known lecture before a Japanese audience delivered in 1978 (the same year as the lecture course *The Birth of Biopolitics*), Foucault imagines what he calls an "analytico-political philosophy," in reference to the Anglo-American tradition of analytic philosophy, which would eschew global theories of power and, instead, would have as its primary task the study of everyday relations of power (i.e., the field of real forces)—as he describes, "a philosophy that would try to demonstrate then source, the forms, the stakes, and the objectives of these power relations."[14] Concerning what he calls the massive qualifications and disqualifications of global structures of power that have preoccupied traditional political philosophy,

> one could say, in a way that is a bit analogous, that in order to analyze or to criticize relations of power it is not a matter of affecting, in a pejorative or laudatory manner, qualifications that are massive, global, and definitive; thus, it's not a question of saying that relations of power can only do one unilateral thing, which is either constraining or repressive. It is no longer even possible to imagine that one could escape the relations of power with one massive and globalizing move, par means of some radical rupture or by some line of flight without return.[15]

The last statement begs the question of whether new political theories of power can be created willy-nilly that will not already be determined to function in some way within the existing institutions and apparatuses of power and, thus, be limited in their ability to effect wholesale transformation of these mechanisms. If subjects are constituted by strategies and already dwell within the historical dispositifs of power relations (of sexuality, discipline, security, territory, populations, etc.), then what is called the field of real forces cannot be viewed from any privileged point of view or agency, and certainly not from a subject of representation, but rather from a series of concerted actions and effects that are primarily historical, social, and impersonal. In other words, the basic problem of "rationalizing power" (that is to say, "the problem of political philosophy over the past five hundred years") is that inevitably, one ends up, sooner or later, *justifying a future system of domination precisely by creating the necessary theory of power to accompany it,* and moreover, a theory that is also *blind to everyday power relations, for the most part, and will not wipe away anyone's tears for too much suffering from power's necessity.*

On a purely discursive level, this assumes a traditional form of ideology by representing a symmetrical relationship between power, right, and truth. Any general theory of power, whether it takes a geometrical, didactic, imperative, moral or political, but especially a juridical form (e.g., the science of jurisprudence), may be deployed for good or ill in different complex situations or according to certain overall strategies in different historical moments. There is no guarantee that the state of affairs that results from a strategic deployment of a system of right in one moment, historically speaking, or for one social situation, will end up creating a better or more just society! In fact, the same system that was originally conceived to justify the overturning of the current arrangement of power relations for a new one can eventually become an oppressive system that deploys violence and war as an essential component of its own right. For example, whether as a tactically effective counterstrategy or a modern theory of Right (what Kant called a "system of justice"), Marxism has occupied both poles in different societies, and there is nothing inherently just or true in any ideology divorced from the concrete social struggles that determine the current power relations. As a general rule, any finite theoretical system can only grasp the future arrangement of power relations on a purely speculative level without resorting to an ideological or mythic representation of history. Likewise, any counterstrategy will often attempt to compensate for the partiality of its viewpoint on the future of power relations by assuming an overtly didactic and ideological form, the form of "scientism" (as in the history of political materialism), or a theological-political or secularized form of utopianism, all of which can be seen in the history of Marxism. (Of course, the same is true for the history of liberalism as well, as we will see in the third section of this chapter.)

THE AXIOMATIC METHOD OF ANALYSIS

The second fundamental problem that we need to address concerning Foucault's method is the subject of experience and the role of natural intuition. If power is neither a substance nor a subject of representation, there can be no presentation of power that could take the form of natural intuition of consciousness. There is no objective perspective or point of view other than a purely theoretical perspective created by the existence of other power relations within the same field of real forces. Why? First, because power is often defined, in its principle, as an a priori analytic concept, or category, which is the philosophical equivalent of an axiom in geometry: the concept contains the predicate, which is declared to be self-evident in the concept. As Descartes defined such immanent representation, "whatever exists as an object of our ideas in a way that exactly matches our perception of it is said to exist *intrinsically* in the object."[16] Kant also insists on the same basic rule in *The Critique of Pure Reason* when he begins the transcendental analytic by first enunciating and then laying out the categories, which are like the geometrical axioms that serve to construct the distinction between a priori analytic and synthetic judgments. For example, Kant says, let the philosopher be given the concept of a triangle, and however hard he may try to analyze it, by examining the more elementary concepts (i.e., line, point, angle, and the number 3), he will never be able to discover in them the property of a triangle as such, that is, of having the sum of its angles equal to two right angles.[17] On the other hand, "if we propose the same question to a geometer, modern or classical, she will construct a triangle by employing a conceptual device and extending one of its sides, then the next, until she arrives at the result through a process of deductive logic that is constantly guided by intuition."[18] And yet, we must ask, where is the "space" of this intuition located except in the figure or "conceptual device" itself and not in natural intuition or empirical consciousness? Omit the construction of a conceptual device, either drawn or imagined, and the presentation itself will collapse into nothingness; therefore it is around this artificial or constructed space that an alternative conclusion can be drawn concerning the role of intuition in certain "spaces" where intuitive representation can hardly be expected.[19] In other words, it is the epiphenomenal manifestation of the idea of "biopower" that is clearly laid out in the analytical construction of the first dispositif, that is to say, appearing as "a complex idea that was formed historically at the interior of the dispositif of sexuality" *(une idée complexe, historiquement formée à l'intérieur du dispositif de sexualité).*[20]

To illustrate this geometric manner, let us now return to the lecture from January 11, 1978, when Foucault returns to the question of method behind his investigations of sexuality, discipline, and security under the general rubric of "biopower." At this point of his analytic, the term is defined as a set of mechanisms that emerged at the moment historically when "Western societies took the basic biological features of the human species as objects of political strategy."[21] What does he say exactly concerning the question of method? First of all, he clarifies that what he is proposing as his guiding terms are hypothetical (i.e., as postulates, to use the geometrical term) and should not be understood as "principles, rules, or theorems."[22] In fact, this is a crucial statement in discerning Foucault's method, since here he evokes the terms of classical Euclidian geometry, even though he poses them negatively at first. Nevertheless, to simply claim on the basis of this statement that Foucault's method is "non-Euclidian," although this may sound appealingly *postmodern*, doesn't explain much, because any method will be groundless unless the reasons for its adoption are given in the presentation of the terms themselves. In fact, the hypothetical function of the postulates must be understood, in relation to a traditional theory of sovereignty or juridical theory of natural right, as what the development of a modern "axiomatized theory" has been to geometry and logic, that is to say, "a system in which the undefined terms and undemonstrated propositions are made completely explicit [at the outset], and the undemonstrated propositions become hypotheses on the basis of which all of the ensuing propositions must be constructed according to explicit rules of the logical order, which must then be demonstrated in the construction of the *machina*."[23]

In classical geometry, a "machine" is merely a conceptual device, drawn or imagined; however, the term *machine* must not be understood mechanistically, at first, but rather as a simple geometrical device (i.e., a figure composed of letters and numbers). According to Euclidian method, first we are given the enunciation of the proposition, then the setting out of the figure and the particular geometrical objects by letters; then comes the definition, which restates the enunciation in terms of the corresponding figure; and finally, the construction of the machinery follows. For example, the solution to the question "what is a triangle?" is already given in the enunciation of the proposition that states that the sum of the angles in every triangle is 180 degrees. However, in the case of the question "what is power?" we have no such initial enunciation, but instead, we have the propositions concerning the specific dispositifs of sexuality or security, for example, and the question of how they function, for what purpose, and at what moment they were invented. However, in the foregoing presentation, it is especially important to remark a change of order, which is nothing less than a change of method. According to a classical method, the construction of the device or machinery follows the definition, and the machinery extends the proof. In Foucault's method, as I will demonstrate in the next section, we have the propositions employed hypothetically in the construction of the conceptual device first, followed by the definitions of how power functions according to the propositions. Thus Foucault places the machinery in the primary position, that is, in place of the definitions or axioms; however, he is not using a form of deductive logic as in geometry because he is not seeking to deduce or demonstrate the existence of eternal forms and ideas but rather to discover the functioning of machinery that has been technically invented and has an efficient causality. For example, the four chapters in the first volume of *The History of Sexuality* list the parameters and the field of strategic reasoning: objective, method, domain, periodization (the last chapter being equivalent to the historical description of a battle waged over the idea of sexuality beginning at some point around the end of the seventeenth century). Foucault's method for describing the new strategies of power is an "axiomatized method" by first asking how power functions across and through institutions and concrete individuals; then by bringing together formerly heterogeneous terms and causing them to be linked together in the propositions concerning how power operates through its historical dispositifs; and finally, in creating or inventing new terms, as well as in defining new forms of subjection.

It is here that we encounter two further problems that may be impossible to resolve: if the dispositifs are patently artificial devices, and thus employed as part of an overall strategy of domination and subjection, then who invented them? History? Society? So-called Man? Certainly not as a subject of Reason, at least, since according to another famous proposition, "Man" only designates the object of a new discursive order of knowledge that is also invented at the end of the seventeenth century. In this regard, we should perhaps recall that Gilles Deleuze often places Kant in the role of creating a "vast and terrible machinery" of the a priori categories (i.e., as axioms in a *more philosophico*), thereby establishing the rules of rationality and the role of the faculties for the next two centuries, and who thus occupies a role in modern philosophy akin to Euclid.[24] According to the logician Robert Blanché, however, the dominance of the Euclidian model of deductive logic is not as much owed to its technical perfection—in fact, many modern logicians have demonstrated its defects—rather, a kind of "applied geometry" was adopted almost universally as a pedagogical tool best suited for disciplining the mind. According to this analogy, this is the role that political philosophy will also assume after Hobbes; its usefulness as a political dispositif is deployed as a "grid of intelligibility" that concretely orders the spaces of the early modern state. In fact, Hobbes developed a new geometry based on the modern science of mechanics, as I will return to discuss in the next section; thus he transformed the geometric method into a general epistemological principle of causality by which, he claimed, we can come to know anything with certainty. "That is the reason why he can claim that we can even come to know the political state by *philosophy*, that is, in a scientific way, namely through causal explanation—because it is produced, generated, or caused by human beings."[25]

As an order of "discipline," therefore, the history of political philosophy might also be understood as an "applied philosophy," something akin to the practical function of Euclidian method as an applied geometry, and this is particularly true in the creation of the science of right and jurisprudence. One begins the analysis of power relations by proposing, as axioms, the form of sovereignty, the centrality of the state-form, and the overall strategy of domination as inherent definitions of power. Its function has heretofore been primarily pedagogical and morally didactic: to rationalize a system of domination by rationalizing power and its effects. This is true whether are talking about the classical philosophy of Machiavelli and Hobbes, the critical philosophy of Kant, or the revolutionary political philosophies of Marx and Engels. Can we imagine, as an alternative, a development similar to that which has taken place in modern geometry and logic, an "axiomatized theory" of politics, or what Foucault himself calls an "analytical-political philosophy"—in other words, a knowledge that would be liberated from this applied and instrumental determination, that would be able to begin to develop models and conceptual devices for understanding power relations that no longer serve to "justify" the permanence of an idea of rationality that is actually based on previous historical arrangements of power and knowledge? Recalling once again the 1978 lecture on "analytical-political philosophy," as Foucault announces, "it is a little bit in this direction that I have been attempting to work [referring to his recent investigations of power] and it is along these lines of research that I would like to indicate a direction we might pursue."[26]

THE RULES OF IMMANENCE

To illustrate this direction, let's return once more to the first presentation of method in volume 1 of *The History of Sexuality* to examine the enunciation of the basic rules and the sequential manner in which they are constructed according to what I have described as an "axiomatized method." Basically, the method has three steps:

(a) to eliminate intuitive meanings of terms so that they don't reoccur tacitly in subsequent reasoning (i.e., sovereignty, the state);
(b) to define terms neutrally as serving no other purpose than to indict the field of relations that occurs in the postulates (i.e., power);
(c) to lay out rules for the construction of models that cannot be achieved by intuition alone (i.e., the concrete dispositifs).

I have already outlined the statements that function to subtract the axioms (or "common notions") that have determined the form, nature, and unity of the traditional representations of sovereign power:

(a) Power is not an ensemble of mechanisms in a state-form (i.e., a machine).
(b) It is not an extended substance or expression of a natural capacity (i.e., sovereign will).
(c) Finally, it is not an overall or unilateral system of domination.

In the next step, the negative statements are then followed by several "undemonstrated propositions," which will function as hypotheses in Foucault's analytic of power. There are four in number:

(a) Power must be understood in the first instance as a multiplicity of force relations immanent in the sphere in which they operate, and which constitute their own organization.
(b) Power must be understood as the process that, through ceaseless struggles and confrontations, transforms, strengthens, or reverses them.

(c) Power must be understood as the support that these force relations find in one another, thus forming a chain or a system, or on the contrary, the disjunctions and contradictions that isolate them from one another.

(d) Finally, only after the first three postulates are demonstrated can one conclude that power must be understood as the strategies whose general design or institutional crystallization are embodied in the state apparatus, in the formulation of the law, in the various social hegemonies.[27]

Here again, we discover the earlier axioms that were subtracted by the initial statements now returning to function hypothetically, which, according to an axiomatized method, cannot be assumed until they are constructed according to the explicit rules of the definitions. Nevertheless, it remains to be seen what logical form these rules will take, and thus what are the concrete rules that guide the construction of the conceptual devices that belong to the demonstration.

Before turning to the four rules, however, which would be the next step in a logical order, Foucault returns once again to enunciate what power is *not,* but in a positive form that is derived from the preceding postulates. Thus, power assumes

(a) the form of a multiplicity;

(b) the nature of a ceaseless struggle from any point in the social field (and not because power is a form that contains all struggles "but because it comes from everywhere");

(c) finally, as produced "from one moment to the next, at every point, or rather in every relation from one point to another."[28]

It is because power relations assume the form of a multiplicity that is produced from every point in the social field that Foucault now introduces a new problem, which is that of perspective or "point of view." However, it is precisely at this point that we find the most well known and most controversial statement in Foucault's entire analytic: if power appears or is produced from every point in the social field, then "its order must not be sought in the primary existence of a central point, in a unique source of sovereignty from which secondary and descendent forms would emanate."[29] In other words, it is here we bear witness to the infamous subtraction of the central perspective, or point of view, as the "condition of possibility" for power to appear as a phenomenon for any empirical subject. From what perspective does power appear? Once again, it is in the "space" of the dispositifs themselves that the phenomenological perception of power first appears in the social field, recalling the earlier description concerning the "complex idea" that was formed historically at the interior of the dispositif of sexuality.

At the same time, it is here we must immediately acknowledge that this also one of the most illogical and even impossible statements in all of Foucault's work. This can be explicitly stated in classical Euclidian terms: power is a sphere without a central point. From a classical geometric understanding, this would be an improper statement or proposition, because a sphere is classically defined as a series of equidistant lines in a three-dimensional space drawn from a central point (i.e., like a circle, which geometrically is an object in two-dimensional space, a sphere is defined mathematically as the set of points that are all at the same distance r from a given point, but in three-dimensional space). From the perspective of a modern theory of the curvature of space, however, it is possible to entertain this proposition simply by subtracting one of the axioms given in the classical Euclidian definition of the sphere, which is not the subtraction of a central point but rather the subtraction of a finite limit, or "limiting surface." Thus, in place of the classical sphere, now we have the conception of an "indefinite sphere" of matter itself, in which the central point can no longer be understood as a fixed point in space (that is, according to the classical Euclidean figure) but rather is extended to every other point by an infinite intensity, *since intensity is to power what density is to matter.* Ultimately, is this not what Foucault is actually describing when he enunciates the "rule of immanence" that determines his own method of representing power relations? Henceforth, "power must not be sought in the primary existence of a central point, in a unique source of sovereignty from which secondary and descendent forms would emanate."[30] Instead, according to Foucault's conclusion that appears in the definitions that follow the postulates, "it is in the area [*champ*] of force relations that we must try to analyze the mechanisms of power; in this way we will escape from the system of Law-and-Sovereign that has captivated political thought for such a long time."[31]

Hence a new definition is provided to determine the value of the central point, which is the definition of sphericity itself, now distributed to every point, perspective, or point of view within the curvature of space that determines the social field *(champ)*. According to the previous figure, sovereignty is the central point that expresses the condition of possibility of all the other points in a spherical form—that is, sovereignty is defined by the power to unify the other points that all intersect through its own limiting surface. According to the new figure of the dispositif, the value of the center now takes the form of an indefinite sphere without a limiting surface or radius. In other words, *intensity is no longer expressed by a central point but rather is extended and is expressed by all the other points in the social field that no longer surround the center but rather constitute either its periphery or its unlimited base.* As a result of this transformation of the classical picture of power relations in a social field defined by sovereignty, the meaning of the central point also fundamentally changes and thus now acquires a new quality of intensity rather than being determined by the quality of extensity that was previously borrowed from the limiting surface. What this demonstrates is that the "common notion" of the central point was essentially an expression of sphericity itself, since even though the center derives all its concentric realities from the sphere in which it becomes an intrinsic term, *the idea of sphericity itself* cannot be confined within its own center—that is, *the center of any sphere does not contain the "idea" of a sphere*! (Basically, this presents us with the same anomaly of the Euclidian model of the sphere that modern geometry discovered at the beginning of the century with the topology of improper or affine spheres.)

In extending this analogy to Foucault's frequent use of geometric figures to present the relations of power (i.e., center, sphere, field or area [*champ*], periphery, limit, etc.), is this not basically the same maneuver that Foucault performs to change the representation of a field of power relations that are organized from every point belonging to the field? That is to say, he changed our mental picture of power relations simply by changing a major rule in the construction of the dominant image of power (or its "common notion") by subtracting a major axiom that determined the previous representation of power (i.e., the central point of sovereignty). Instead of a circle or a sphere with a central point, "power must be understood in the first instance [in its principle] as a multiplicity of force relations immanent in the sphere [*au domaine*] in which they operate, and which constitutes their own organization."[32] Moreover, these relations are now said to be immanent to one another so that there is no point that is exterior to another within the field, and certainly no point of view exterior to the field itself from which to grasp all the interior points in the form of a unity, whether that of a structure, a system, or even a single mechanism (a "machine" or "apparatus" [*appareil*]).

With this last definition, I believe we have discovered both conditions for the variety and the multiplicity of the modern dispositifs of power; at the same time, we have glimpsed the condition of real social space itself. In other words, because social space is, at each and every point, already subjectively predisposed and spatially prearranged by preexisting power relations—on both a global level addressed to populations and also on an individual level, and even on a subindividual or micropolitical level—*the plane that embodies real social space is always already curved.*

But what exactly does the "curvature" of real social space mean in this sense? In fact, it has five senses:

(a) According to the first sense (i.e., subjective), real social space is curved in such a manner that two subjects can occupy external positions in space that are relatively near to one another and yet never meet on the same line, or the same point, since a third line runs through these points that is fundamentally fractured or cut, constituting the form of intersubjectivity that is ordered by language and representation.

(b) According to the second sense (i.e., objective), real social space is curved in a Kantian sense of infinite representation in the idea of a Whole that can never be totalized in one representation, that is, in a synthetic or a posteriori representation of a manifold.

(c) According to the third sense (i.e., dynamic), real social space is curved in the sense that the subjective positions in social space are already arranged or ordered by overall strategies and by concrete assemblages (*les agencements concretes)* and by the historical dispositifs of preexisting power relations.

(d) According to the fourth sense (i.e., strategic or nonapodictic), real social space is curved since there is no neutral or objective point of view that has not already been historically conditioned by these concrete assemblages of power relations.

(e) Finally, according to the fifth sense (i.e., historico-political), real social space can be defined as having the characteristic of being curved by the most generalized form of strategic intentionality that appears to determine the nature of power relations that belong to each historical epoch.

According the last definition, the true distinction between power and knowledge would lie somewhere between the most general and the most strategic intentionality for power and the domain and duration (i.e., space and time) where these strategies are manifested within concrete mechanisms and tactics, namely, in the dispositifs of sexuality, biopower, security, territory, and so on. Ultimately, there can be no ontological representation of power (i.e., *no theory of power*), because there can be no distance from which "power" itself could be grasped in the form of a quasi-scientific or even "theoretical" objectivity. Instead, Foucault transforms the pre-ontological character of general intentionality in phenomenology by introducing the terms *strategy* and *strategic*. As a result of this transformation or reversal, which I address in Article III, the ontological character of transcendental intentionality assumes an essentially strategic definition, and at the same time, the practical notion of strategy is generalized and dispersed throughout the social field, because there is no longer one subjective form of power. In fact, it is precisely this transcendent perspective that is subtracted from Foucault's analysis to grasp the reality of the social space as always already constituted by power relations, even though these relations are not yet determined by any specific form, thereby producing the effect of multiplicity. This is why subjectivity is now apprehended from a multiplicity of perspectives that are constituted by real power relations; accordingly, power can no longer be viewed from the ideal perspective (or "point of view") of a form that unifies, centralizes, or totalizes the entire social field.

The idea of power as an immanent field of strategies perhaps constitutes Foucault's most radical proposition, because this implies that power has no natural ontological representation. Moreover, if power has no proper ontological or a priori form, then it also follows that it can undergo historical modulation in its different a posteriori representations—i.e., in one historical epoch, it can appear in the form of an organism; in the next, as a machine; and in the third, as a structure. For example, as we will see in the next part, was it not when the idea of power assumed a mechanistic and thermodynamic formal ontology that the idea of the state suddenly refashioned itself into the most modern understanding of an apparatus or machine? What is also crucial to notice in the preceding descriptions of real social space as a manifold of relations (i.e., immanence, continuity, contiguity) is that it is not already structured into a hierarchy or pyramid (although, as Deleuze will later observe, "no doubt the pyramidal will subsist, but with a function that is diffuse and spread all over its surfaces"). For example, the relation of verticality (or the relation between dominator and dominated) will always be a feature of social space, but power does not flow in one direction only (i.e., "from above") but also simultaneously emerges "from below," especially because the subjugated or dominated also produce the reality of the perspective of the dominator as an explanation of how power functions. As Foucault argues (a bit like Spinoza did before him), power continuously invests in and depends on the "inadequate ideas" of those whom it subjugates, since it is only by means of this *conatus* that it can pass through them as if helped along by the representation of the subjugated bodies that undergo its effects. Without any knowledge of its own effects, which will serve as the content of future stratagems, in addition to being blind, power would remain a virtual play of forces that would obtain no subjective form of knowledge. It is this insight that leads Foucault to focus on what he calls "subjugated knowledges" in the earlier works from the 1970s onward.

In the 1972 interview conducted by Deleuze called "Intellectuals and Power," Foucault defines the relationship between a general theory—I have preferred the term "a general strategy" in keeping with his later formulation—and a specific "struggle" in the same topological terms that will be also be employed in first defining the nature of the dispositif in *The History of Sexuality.* "A Theory is the regional system of a particular struggle." Moreover, "each struggle develops from a particular *foyer* of power [I prefer to leave this French term untranslated]; one of these innumerable and small *foyers* which can be a boss, a guardian of the HLM, a director of the prison, a judge, a responsible syndicate, the editor in chief of a newspaper or journal."[33]

The term *foyer* is interesting when employed in Foucault's description of "local," "specific," even "singular," sites where general strategies are actualized in terms of both theory and practice. Apart from designating an architectural space outside the enclosure of a house or domicile, the topological definition of the foyer is a conical section where there is a constant distance maintained between each of the points of a curve in relation to a fixed angle or direction. In the French, the term *foyer* also designates the point from which something first arrives, as in the outbreak of a contagion or an epidemic. Both definitions help to clarify Foucault's use of the term to designate the virtual position from which a political strategy first emerges from a specific site of struggle or subjectivity, and toward which this strategy is directed or oriented across social relations, attempting to unify them in an immanent form of movement and direction (i.e., "a collective struggle"). In the preceding passage, we see that the *foyer* (or focal point) is occupied in each case by a personage of authority or power (e.g., a boss, a guardian, a prison director, a judge). As a topological figure, the collective subjectivity that belongs to a local strategy first emerges as being opposite and external to this location in social space, and the different members of the struggle could be defined as the equidistant points in the curvature of space. But in what direction are these points moving, and why does subjectivity appear at an exterior point of the structure or apparatus?

To take a concrete example that forms the context of the interview, prisoners revolt against the conditions of the prison and take as their target the authority of the director (or warden), who functions precisely as a focal point for organizing their struggle, that is, for arranging themselves in a collective made up of equidistant points of subjectivity. Of course, the prisoners are certainly no dupes, and they already know that the director does not occupy the central point of the apparatus. He did not create the prison, and behind the director is a series of other subjects and mechanisms, including the administrators and judges, the penal code, the legislative body, and even the state apparatus itself. This topology is perfectly illustrated in Kafka's short parable "Before the Law," when the doorkeeper says, "I am powerful. But I am the least of the doorkeepers. From hall to hall there is one doorkeeper after another, each more powerful than the last. Third doorkeeper is already so terrible that even I cannot bear to look at him."[34]

As in the case of the many concrete struggles we have recently witnessed—even participated in—eventually, all these points will be connected in a larger and expanding topology of the social and institutional spaces that these various personages occupy, like a conical section of a diagram with an open base or summit. At each phase of the local struggle, the subjects will need to include these other points and personages in a general strategy (as a partial component or "theory" of their practice) and, at the same time, maintain the general form of subjectivity as the equidistant points that are uniform in relation to a focal point that is always pushed outward until it encompasses the entire social space itself to the point of saturating the social field with its own power relation like a colorist in painting. Historically, feminism has been successful in totalizing the social field in this manner; more recently, the expression of Black Lives Matter and the subjects of disability and LGBTQ have effectively reoriented the entire social field from a particular point of view or concrete struggle. What we are witnessing in both these examples, according to Foucault's early description of a struggle, is a dynamic representation of the birth of a new subjective form of resistance and new connections in real social space that are all linked through the different points of exteriority, from *foyer* to *foyer*, expanding to the periphery of the social field as such. The interiority or central point is never reached, however, because there is no central focal point in social space itself; rather, the interiority is projected by subjectivity as a purely virtual point to orient external movement through real social space.

Perhaps now we are in a better position to grasp a major principle behind what I am calling Foucault's "geometric manner": to change our understanding of power requires nothing less than to change the order of the elements that informed its previous representations. Second, to change this order requires a new method and a new manner of representing social space itself, which functions by subtracting the axioms or by adding new rules for constructing the diagrams. Third, this also means changing the logical form that defines all its elements and their meaning (the central point, the limiting surface or radius, the multiplicity of points connected to the radius, etc.). At the same time, to simply change or subtract a major rule or axiom exposes the diagram itself to collapsing into an illogical form of impossibility and threatens the previous representation of power in the same way that if you remove a central motor from a machine, the machine will no longer function. Is this not also what happens when the virtual nexus that was provided by the previous dispositif of sovereign or state power can no longer be mapped onto real social space, according to Foucault's hypothesis, and suddenly the symmetrical and unified picture of power relations threatens to collapse into a chaos of multiple relations without perspective or order, in which "a mobile perspective is produced from one moment to the next, at every point, or rather in every relation from one point to another"?[35] Not only is this definition illogical according to the rules that have long been accepted in representing power relations in a three-dimensional social space (which I have already compared to the continued authority of Euclidian geometry) but the introduction of this mobile perspective has even been viewed by some as a dangerous threat to the symmetrical ordering of power relations between height and base, center and periphery, interior and exterior, and so on.

Therefore it is not at all surprising that for the last forty years or so, many of Foucault's historical critics and recent interlocutors have sought precisely to restore the classical diagram of sovereign power by rectifying his own descriptions of how power also works through the invention of new technical dispositifs and concrete tactics. In most cases, they have corrected his diagrams either by restoring the axiomatic function of the central point (e.g., the "blind spot" in Foucault's own theory) or by reasserting the relation of verticality as an essential attribute that conditions all power relations (in the manner of an axiom that defines the subject of power). As a perspective or imaginary "point of view," power only belongs to those who are already identified to possess it from a perspective of a given social field. I am not implying that these critics are imagining things or that they are simply carrying old snapshots of power in their heads—perhaps in a similar way to which Deleuze and Guattari once complained that people also had trees growing in their heads—because we have already established that the perception of power does not take place in mental representation alone but rather is a "complex idea" that must first grow inside the concrete dispositif where subjectivity also resides.

Regarding the persistence of the pyramidal form, as Foucault argues in *Discipline and Punish*, "power in the hierarchical surveillance of the disciplines is not possessed as a thing or transferred as a property; it functions like a piece of machinery [*machinerie*]. And, although it is true that its pyramidal organization gives it a head, it is the apparatus [*appareil*] as a whole that produces power and distributes individuals in this permanent and continuous field."[36] However, contrary to what many critics have understood Foucault actually to be saying (i.e., that the earlier dispositifs of sovereignty and discipline have vanished and we are now living in the age of "biopower"), I will approach this claim more cautiously. The very fact that sovereign and disciplinary power are still apprehended as ideas that continue to inform the social field means that these ideas still *function* as pieces of a vast machinery that produces the reality of power relations today. In other words, *it is only the nature of the dispositif itself that has changed, and thus the question concerning the "apparatus" that produces power and distributes individuals throughout the social field is the subject of my analysis.* To understand the technical differences between the terms *machinerie, appareil,* and *dispositif,* it is precisely this transcendent perspective that is subtracted from Foucault's analysis to grasp the reality of the social space as always already constituted by power relations, even though these relations are not yet determined by any specific form, thereby producing the effect of multiplicity. Consequently, in the next part, we will need to trace the genealogy of their first appearance in Foucault's analysis by returning once more to an age-old question: what is a dispositif?

2. Conceptual Device

To begin the analysis of the genealogy of the concept of dispositif, I will lay out two preliminary propositions:

(a) *Proposition 1: Concepts are not defined by propositions; they do not exist in dictionaries. Demonstration*: Concepts are defined by statements, and new statements can suddenly change the meaning of an earlier concept, as in the case of the concept of the "apparatus" *(appareil)*, which is suddenly redefined by a new term Foucault introduces to designate his own concept of "dispositif." One result of the introduction of this new term is that it causes the concept of apparatus to undergo a sudden reversal between interior and exterior, because apparatuses will now be found to be interior to so-called dispositifs, but without reconstituting a new form of interiority. In keeping with this sense of conceptual reversal, I would argue that the exact status of Foucault's term is that it is a neologism. In other words, he invented the term to (1) avoid using another term that was already coupled to the term *appareil* (i.e., *machine*) and (2) to invest the term with an innovative and more general sense that would be the basis for his own analysis of power, but only as a result of further demonstration of the alternative political and technical dispositifs. Of course, some readers might object to my use of the term as a neologism for a term that already existed in the French lexicon, which already possessed a definite semantic content and etymological history. Nevertheless, the fact that a word exists in a language does not convey its usage, the frequency of its uses, and in what contexts the word is employed. Moreover, given the fact that the word was not employed previously in the same theoretical context as the term *appareil* (Althusser), the introduction of the term *dispositif* as a conceptual discussion at this point in the history of the discourse on power would give Foucault the distinctive advantage of also redefining its conceptual cousin.

(b) *Proposition 2: Concepts are not defined in isolation as units of meaning. Demonstration*: Concepts are defined in the context of other terms to which they are related or opposed (much like synonyms or antonyms) or serve as qualifiers. For this reason, the meaning of the word *dispositif* cannot be defined apart from or outside the history of statements that earlier defined the term *appareil* (and now, as a result of Foucault's neologism, vice versa). As Foucault already argues in *The Archeology of Knowledge,* words only occur in statements, and new statements that define a term's meaning appear in the present and can suddenly transform the entire sense of what the term designates; thus "the statement is not the same kind of unit as the sentence, the proposition, or the speech act; it cannot be referred therefore to the same criteria; but neither is it the same kind of unit as the material object, with its limits and independence."[1] This is how I would also understand the object of the statement, or rather the questions, What is an apparatus? What is a dispositif? after Foucault's first usage of the term beginning in 1975. The basic distinction between what is called an apparatus and what is called a dispositif can be defined depending on what lexicon one chooses to represent "a device" or "a mechanism" that literally causes (i.e., "makes ready") an order of power to appear—sexuality, sovereignty, discipline, security, control, and so on.

In 1988 and in 2006, respectively, Gilles Deleuze and Giorgio Agamben each addressed this term in essays that both bear the same question as their title. Both philosophers generally agree that the term refers to the heterogeneous mechanisms of "capturing" and "transforming" living beings into subjects in the process of which a "dimension of power" plays a crucial role.[2] They also emphasized the plurality of these "mechanisms," thus referring not to a single dispositif (or "ideological apparatus," as in previous Marxist theory) but rather to the "multilinear skein" or ensemble of disciplinary mechanisms of subjection and new "modal processes of subjectivization" *(modes d'asujettissement).*[3] One might argue, however, that both Deleuze and Agamben provide a purely formal diagram or onto-logical image of power rather than going through the pains of a concrete analysis of the inner workings of the historical mechanisms of power and discipline. For example, as visual theorist Olga Bryukhovetska has pointed out, the only example given by Agamben (i.e., the alienating power of cel-lular phones) bears all the pitfalls of technological determinism: "In this case, what is called a dispositif becomes a kind of all-embracing network of oppressive 'social machines' intermingled with technophobic fantasy—a power matrix from which no subject can escape."[4]

Agamben derives the term *dispositif* exclusively from the ecclesiastical and Latin term *dispositio* (i.e., the instrument and governance of human history by Christ). Of course, this is not the first time that he substitutes one language for another—Latin for French—or a Roman Catholic gene-alogy for a Greek or modern one. In some ways, this constitutes Agamben's own particular conceptual device or "writing machine." I would simply point out his main argument, drawn from Schmitt's political theology, that political and juridical concepts are simply religious concepts that have be-come secularized through modernity. Thus Agamben's own "method" is to *re-ligio* (to "rebind") political concepts to their purported original religious sources.[5]

To his credit, Deleuze was the first to emphasize the "artificial unity" that determines the heterogeneous nature of Foucault's concept. "First of all," he writes,

> it is a skein, a multilinear whole. It is composed of lines of different na-tures. The lines of a dispositif do not encircle or surround systems that are each homogenous to themselves, the object, the subject, language, etc. [i.e., the dispositif is not a structure, a machine, an organic system], but follow directions, trace processes that are always out of balance, that sometimes move closer together and sometimes farther away.[6]

Nevertheless, in the preceding definition, we are simply offered the propo-sition of a "multilinear whole" and then told what it is not—that is, it is not a form of encirclement, or a container for a homogenous system in which the elements are enclosed inside like cogs in a machine—and defines something that is in perpetual motion, in a constant state of disequilibrium or in a state of contraction or expansion. Of course, there are philosophi-cal analogues that display similar characteristics (e.g., Leibniz's concept of monad, Bergson's concept of duration), but the simplest analogy that Deleuze offers is a Riemannian patch of space-time itself.[7] This definition is also given in the first section of *Foucault,* titled "A New Cartographer," where Deleuze writes, "The thing called power is characterized by immanence of field without transcendent unification, continuity of line without global centralization, and contiguity of parts without distinct totalization: i.e., it is social space."[8]

And yet, we come back to my earlier question: What kind of form or set of relations does this describe? That is to say, from what model or figure is it drawn? Mathematics? Geometry? Architecture? Informatics? Archeology? Taxonomy? Cartography? (The last two are most likely, because these are the disciplines Deleuze explicitly identifies with Foucault's method—"a new archivist, a new cartographer.") In my opinion, what Deleuze is actually providing is an analogue to his own concept of the "rhizome," which is described in exactly the same characteristics: an uneven mixture of connection and multiplicity (i.e., "a skein, a multilinear whole"), varieties of measurement without unity, an essentially heterogeneous reality composed of broken lines and discontinuous ruptures. My intention is not to fault Deleuze, much less dismiss his definition as impure, because he is simply confronting the nature of Foucault's concept and attempting to describe it according to its own peculiar characteristics, but in the end, he inevitably falls back on his own resources, his own imagination, that is to say, his own concepts which function as analogues (the "Body without Organs," the "rhizome," the "Assemblage," etc.). However, because we cannot take these descriptions to stand for the same concept that Foucault defines, we must follow closely Foucault's own descriptions and provisionally (if not permanently) abandon the ones provided by Agamben and Deleuze.

Let us now turn to the conceptual cousin, apparatus *(appareil),* by sticking as close as possible to the French etymology, which is certainly a source that Foucault himself employed. In fact, this will be the same source that Althusser employs to define the conceptual couple *"appareil-machine"* in the lectures from the late 1960s that were later published in *Marx dans ses limites* (1978).[9] Turning to *Robert,* it is interesting to find that the first definition of the term *appareil* is one that seldom appears in most discussions of the concept that determine it from a mechanistic or machinic metaphor; instead, it refers to the "unfolding of a ceremonial procession in the eyes of the spectators (e.g., a funeral procession, or mass)."[10] For example, the royal robe of a king is an apparatus, as well as the crown and the scepter, which are part of the ceremonial and ritual presentation of the sovereign's power. Thus, robe, crown, and scepter can be defined as elements of a ritual and ceremonial apparatus for producing the visible appearance of power. The coronation of the king is a ritual apparatus *(appareil)* composed of several elements in a moving presentation that "makes visible" *(appaittre),* "brings to appearance" *(apparition),* and even "makes apparent" *(apparent)* the sovereign power. In each sense, the term *appareil* has for its direct root the middle French present active infinitive *apparaitre,* but also the noun *apparat,* meaning a pompous or solemn occasion. But this comes as a quite a surprise given that this derivation seems to have completely dropped out of any usual definition of the term *apparatus.*

Why is this so, especially given that this etymological relation is so self-evident and immediately visible? Was it because no one had thought to mention it, or because it was self-evident that one merely assumed that everyone knew the verbal connection? Was it because the sense of spectacle that defines the closest French term, *apparat,* was too theatrical, or the ritual sense of the term too religious and ceremonial (i.e., archaic) to render its distinctly modern sense, especially after the word *apparatus* began to be employed more frequently in English after 1820, and in French after 1920? Or rather, was it because the mechanical or machinic association was more easily derived from the Latin *apparare* (to make ready), which was more in keeping with its modern usage? In other words, perhaps this suspicious absence of the term's primary meaning can be explained simply by referring to the evolution of the technology of the state form for displaying or making visible its power and even demonstrates one of the most striking semantic and phenomenological transformations of the idea of the modern state, which begins to be imagined or thought of as a machine beginning sometime in the eighteenth century after Hobbes (as Foucault might say with characteristic flourish). Of course, the association of the state as a "machine," or the representation of the state as a kind of mechanism, is not a natural association but a historical one that is later categorically insisted upon by the time of Marx and Lenin. Prior to the eighteenth century, however, the state was more associated or metaphorically represented as an organism or particularly associated with the body, as Foucault had demonstrated earlier in *Discipline and Punish*.

Returning now to the mechanical and most literal definition of *appareil* as "device," here it is important to note that this normally does not refer to any device but specifically to a device that has moving parts and a motor (e.g., *appareil de photo,* or "camera"). Thus it is here we find the equivalence between an apparatus and a machine. As Althusser argues, both Marx and Lenin insist upon the terms *appareil-machine* in reference to the entity of the state and even exclusively reserve these two terms only for this "special machine."[11] However, as we will see in the next section, the problem with Althusser's concept device of the apparatus is that he has to resort to a reproduction of the modern notion of mechanism to define its principle as already that of the "function" that belongs to the order of modern machines. Thus the apparatus is already determined as part of a more general order to which its function is assigned to the superstructure, and the primary term belongs to the mode of production. This leads to a tautology in the concept itself, which is why Althusser must resort to defining certain state apparatuses as repressive, directly subjecting the body to power or force (the police, the prison, the army), while others are defined as ideological-*appareil,* whose form of subjection is imaginary, producing in the consciousness of the subject a correlate of the subjected body in the form of an identity, which Foucault refers to later as a kind of "autonomous docility."[12] It is this concept of the apparatus that is earlier employed in *Discipline and Punish,* which is early on taken from Marx and defined as a homogenous assemblage or "machine."

But it is also important to point out that this is where the notion of a general strategy of warfare that is also applied to populations and to the individual body through the technique of politics and the economic division of labor first appears as well. In the lectures of the same year, however, Foucault's understanding of mechanism is gradually derived more from Canguilhem, who in turn finds it first in Descartes. As Canguilhem argues, for example, the emergence of capitalism is not the result of the fixed ratio of labor time as from the prior disposition of the parts themselves. Thus it is only on the basis of this prior disposability of parts that the entire process can be standardized and numerically determined—that is, the parts or elements must be homogenized. The soul cannot move the body unless the different parts that compose a body are already predisposed to move in union; likewise, an army, which is assembled from heterogeneous elements, cannot move as one body unless they are already made from the same *mettle*. As Foucault writes,

> hence the need to find a whole calculated practice of individual and collective dispositions, movements of groups or isolated elements, changes of position, of movement from one disposition to another; in short, the need to invent a machinery whose principle would no longer be the mobile or immobile mass, *but a geometry of divisible segments whose basic unity was the mobile soldier with his rifle*; and, no doubt, below the soldier himself, the minimal gestures, the elementary stages of actions, the fragments of spaces occupied or traversed.[13]

It is at this moment that we find the convergence of two techniques that will later be employed to define the dual object of the biopolitical order: strategies of war directed at the level of populations and concrete tactics directed at the level of the individual body, and, finally, even below the individual body defined both as a substance and as a minimal unit of calculation in an overall strategy, directly at the elements and forces of life itself. This distinction between the overall strategy and the various concrete tactics and techniques invented to shape and condition the possibilities of living will determine the nexus of macro- and micro-perspectives of the biopolitical order and, henceforth, the dual object of the government of living bodies, which I will return to discuss in greater detail later in this chapter.

For now, this dual perspective of power is why I have argued that Foucault selects the term *dispositif*, in part to avoid using other terms that are already coupled with the concept of the apparatus, which are machine, structure, system, and organism. Each of these forms requires a homogenous space and determines the elements of parts of any ensemble. Once again, power is neither a machine, an organism, nor a structure. In geometrical terms, these are merely "common notions" that belong to a historical stage of technological modernization. Foucault, in effect, deregulates this machine analogy by removing what is the essential element of all three: a homogenous space and time internal to the function, a standardization of its terms or parts, whether this is understood as linguistic elements in a structure, or mechanical parts in a machine, or component parts of an apparatus or an organism. For example, there is no structure in which all the elements that supposedly belong to the structure would be absolutely heterogeneous to one another; likewise, there is no machine that is composed of absolutely heterogeneous parts. In each case, the elements would be external to the form of a structure or the function of a machine, and there would be no homogenous and interior relation (i.e., the elements would not belong to the structure, the parts would not belong to the machine). And yet, is this exteriority itself a new form of relation, without becoming yet again another structure?

Nevertheless, this seems to be what Foucault is suggesting by the term. Otherwise, why does Foucault insist on the heterogeneity of assemblage of elements, except to define an order that no longer can be determined mechanistically, that is, as parts of a machine? It is equally interesting to point out that Foucault makes no reference to Althusser's earlier and very influential usage of the term *dispositif*. Perhaps this is for the same reasons that mark the distinction that Foucault introduces in his own discussion of the disciplinary mechanism, which avoids any mechanical analogy to the state apparatus as an outmoded and historical model of power relations centered on the "administrative machinery of control."[14] (I will return to this analogy again in article III, concerning what he calls later on the "inflationary theory of the state form" in many post–World War II critical theories of the Left.) Given that Foucault was Althusser's former student, it seems improbable that he was not familiar with Althusser's writings on the French terms *appareil* and *dispositif*, particularly since they are published in the same period as *The History of Sexuality* and the 1975 lecture of January 15, when the term *dispositif* appears for the very first time around the technique of "normalization" in the government of living beings.[15] Although the study of this technique is first applied to the domain of sexuality in the same year, Foucault suggests that it can be extrapolated as a general (or "typical") technique of the exercise of power "that can be transferred to many different institutions and apparatuses."[16]

In the lectures, Foucault first explains the process of normalization by applying Canguilhem's groundbreaking interpretation from *The Normal and the Pathological* (1966), where the power of the norm is first defined as something that operates differently from law, since the norm's function is not to exclude and reject but rather is always linked to a positive technique of intervention and transformation, to a sort of normative project that is invested directly in the field of social and biopolitical forces.[17] Thus a model of biological normalization is substituted for mechanical causality to determine the evolutionary path of any normative order as also being open to the moments of rupture and discontinuity or, at least, the sudden appearance of new elements and techniques as part of a generalized struggle of an organism to maintain its consistency and overall unity. For Canguilhem, the unity of the organism in its encounter with the environment can only be defined as a constant agnostic struggle. For example, in its encounter with illness, the organism attempts to invent a new norm that will be able to maintain its integrity and restore balance in its relation to its environment—both interior and exterior.[18]

At this point, we should now reply to the question "what is a dispositif?" by simply calling it the idea of a generalized strategy, that is, according to Foucault's own claim that the general technique of power is by nature essentially strategic, and thus, in the beginning of the eighteenth century, power is defined by its strategic aims, both in war and in politics.[19] But what is a strategy? A strategy can be defined as a line of force that is exterior to the elements but assembles them in a certain order and according to a certain end. In politics, as in war, for example, in the multiple relations of force that are formed and operate in the apparatuses (appareils) of production, a general line of force traverses local battles and links them together. To illustrate this, let us think of the difference between war and battle. A battle is a finite instance that reproduces the general conflict, as well as the terms and subjects of this conflict. But the outcome of the battle does not necessarily determine the end of the war; the battle moves the war further along, extends the process, until the next instance. The winner and the loser will assess the outcome of the battle as part of a general strategy to win the war, but the war is not over until the conditions of reproduction on one side are reduced to a point where one can no longer go on fighting. By choosing the term dispositif, however, Foucault disregards the mechanistic definition of an apparatus and chooses instead its secondary meaning: the ensemble of military pieces disposed according to a strategic plan.

Later, in the same argument, Foucault summarizes this analogy in a manner that will continue to inform the thesis that in the modern period, politics becomes increasing made up of strategies and tactics that are derived from the technologies of warfare. Moreover, what is the most generalized strategy except the subjection of one force by another force in a field of real and multiple force relations? For Foucault, what is new in the "generalized strategy of subjection" is that the exercise of force does not only occur through repression or cancellation of the force but also by incitement, provocation, intensification, and seduction. So, as he announces his intention in the conclusion of the lecture course of January 15, 1975, during the period he was also researching the first dispositif of sexuality, "I will try and employ this positive conception of power when analyzing how, from the 17th to the end of the 19th century, normalization was attempted in the domain of sexuality."[20]

THE "DEPLOYMENT" OF SEXUALITY

So far, I have insisted on an essentially strategic use, let us say invention, of the term *dispositif* to avoid three other terms that have been employed in the history of the concept of power that was defined by a metaphorical equivalent or analogy; these terms are *machine, structure,* and *organism.* In other words, for Foucault, a dispositif is neither a machine, nor a structure, nor finally an organism, even though it can contain and express all of these as elements in a general strategy of power. Moreover, following the temporality of the norm in Canguilhem, *the emergence of a historical dispositif is existentially prior, but ontologically second in order of appearance* (echoing Heidegger's ontic-ontological difference in phenomenology), which is why I have chosen to derive its specific mode of appearance from the Latin term *appārēscō* (and not by the ecclesiastical term *dispositio,* which is derived from the Hellenic *oikonomia,* meaning "administration").[21] Therefore, as I will repeat throughout the course of this study, what is called "a dispositif" can better be understood as a "conceptual device" that specifically causes something *to begin to appear,* and perhaps this gives the term a more historical and less ontologically inflected meaning, as if the "form of power" itself undergoes an ontological modulation or *molting.* Consequently, it is also crucial to observe that, later, Foucault will reject any serialization of the various dispositifs he defines, beginning with sexuality. Thus, in the lecture of January 11, 1978, Foucault cautions that in his account, "there is not a series of successive elements, the appearance of the new causing the previous ones to disappear."

There is not a legal age, the disciplinary age, and then an age of security [i.e., an age of biopolitics]. Mechanisms of security do not replace disciplinary mechanisms [thus, control does not follow discipline, as I will demonstrate later on], which would have replaced juridical-legal mechanisms [i.e., mechanisms of sovereignty]. In reality you have a series of complex edifices in which, of course, the techniques themselves change and are perfected, or anyway become more complicated, but in which what above changes is the dominant characteristic, or more exactly, the system of correlation between juridical-legal mechanisms, disciplinary mechanisms, and mechanisms of security. In other words, there is a history of the actual techniques themselves.[22]

To my knowledge, Foucault himself directly addressed his use of the term *dispositif* only once during a roundtable discussion that also took place in 1977, which I quote here at length:

What I'm trying to pick out with this term is, firstly, a thoroughly heterogeneous ensemble consisting of discourses, institutions, architectural forms, regulatory decisions, laws, administrative measures, scientific statements, philosophical, moral and philanthropic propositions—in short, the said as much as the unsaid. Such are the elements of the dispositif. The dispositif itself is the system of relations that can be established between these elements. Secondly, what I am trying to identify in this dispositif is precisely the nature of the connection that can exist between these heterogeneous elements. Thus, a particular discourse can figure at one time as the program of an institution, and at another it can function as a means of justifying or masking a practice which itself remains silent, or as a secondary re-interpretation of this practice, opening out for it a new field of rationality. In short, between these elements, whether discursive or non-discursive, there is a sort of interplay of shifts of position and modifications of function which can also vary very widely. Thirdly, I understand by the term dispositif a sort of—shall we say—formation which has as its major function at a given historical moment that of responding to an urgent need. The dispositif thus has a dominant strategic function. This may have been, for example, the assimilation of a floating population found to be burdensome for an essentially mercantilist economy: there was a strategic imperative acting here as the matrix for a dispositif which gradually undertook the control or subjection of madness, sexual illness and neurosis.[23]

To illustrate his description, let us take the first concrete dispositif that Foucault analyzes, the "dispositif of sexuality" (from chapter 4 of the first volume of *The History of Sexuality*):

(a) First, beginning in the nineteenth century, there is a concerted elaboration of the idea of sexuality as something that is not anatomically determined by biology, but rather is discovered to have intrinsic properties and laws of its own, properties and laws that were formerly either repressed or shrouded in a secrecy that now promises to define the essence of Man.

(b) Second, as Foucault alludes here to the early birth of the clinic, this undiscovered continent of sexuality is immediately coupled with a concrete strategy of "hystericizing" the subject of woman, which produces three kinds of sexuality: biologically and anatomically, as that which belongs in common to men and women; culturally, as that which belongs, par excellence, to men, and hence is lacking in women; pathologically, pertaining to the specific physiology of women, as that which by itself constitutes woman's body, ordering it wholly in terms of the functions of reproduction and keeping it in constant agitation through the effects of that very function.

(c) Next, third, from this strategy there follows a consequent hystericizing of children, which was deployed by Freud and his followers in the interpretation of the perversions as the latent sexuality of the child that would later reappear in adult life as the effects of the premature and incomplete sexualization, the theoretical basis for understanding and classifying the modern neuroses.

(d) Finally, fourth, the idea of "sex" is given a universal and cosmological signification as the expression of the polarity of Thanatos–Eros, or the economic determination of the drives and the constant tendency of the pleasure principle to elude this grid of economic determinism.[24]

In each of these strategic significations, Foucault gives us a vivid description of the concrete dispositif of sexuality, which is initially defined as an "artificial unity" of heterogeneous elements in more generalizable strategies of subjection and subjectification:

(a) First, the notion of "sex" made it possible to group together, in an *artificial unity,* anatomical elements, biological functions, conducts, sensations, and pleasures; it enabled one to make use of this fictitious unity as a causal principle, an omnipresent meaning, a secret to be discovered everywhere: sex was thus able to function as a unique signifier and as a universal signified.

(b) Second, by presenting itself in a unitary fashion, as anatomy and lack, as function and latency, as instinct and meaning, the idea of sex was able to mark the line of contact between a knowledge of human sexuality and the biological sciences of reproduction; thus, without really borrowing anything from these sciences, excepting a few doubtful analogies, the knowledge of sexuality gained through proximity a guarantee of quasi-scientificity.

(c) Third, according to Foucault, the idea of sex brought about a fundamental reversal; it made it possible to invert the representation of the relationships of power to sexuality, causing the latter to appear [or to begin to appear] not in its essential and positive relation to power, but as being rooted in a specific and irreducible urgency which power tries as best it can to dominate; thus the idea of "sex" makes it possible to evade what gives "power" its power; it enables one to conceive power solely as law and taboo.[25]

"Sex," henceforth, is "that [hidden] agency which appears to dominate us and that secret which seems to underlie all that we are, that point which enthralls us through the power it manifests and the meaning it conceals, and which we ask to reveal what we are and to free us from what defines us."[26] As Foucault observes, "it is doubtless an ideal point was made necessary by the 'deployment' [*dispositif*] of sexuality and its operation," at this point referring to the function of its conceptual device in shaping the social idea of sexuality that is born at this moment historically. However, he immediately qualifies the nature of this function (i.e., the notion of mechanism underlying the notion of an apparatus) by saying that "we must not make the mistake of thinking that sex is an *autonomous agency* [m.e.] which secondarily produces manifold effects of sexuality over the entire length of its surface of contact with power," recalling the earlier passage that locates its appearance as "a complex idea that was formed historically at the interior of the dispositif" (*ou bien une idée complexe, historiquement formée à l'intérieur du dispositif*).[27] Consequently, as a result, "sex is the most speculative, most ideal, and most internal element in a deployment [*dispositif*] of sexuality organized by power in its grip on bodies and their materiality, their forces, energies, sensations, and pleasures."[28]

I have quoted extensively from these passages because I think they vividly demonstrate the material creation of sexuality as the domain of the first dispositif that Foucault uncovers. Its practical and theoretical function is to project an imaginary point in the deployment of the relation to power that the individual has to pass through to have access to the "complex idea" of his own intelligibility as a person, including access to his own sexualized body and subjective identity. (Of course, as Foucault also adds, the irony of this deployment is in making us believe that our liberation was in the balance.)[29] Foucault will return to this hypothesis in 1982, two years before his death, to announce a new problem of power that concerns precisely the explosion of new forms of subjectification, in some sense echoing his earlier observations regarding a similar explosion of new disciplinary techniques at the end of the eighteenth century. Although the struggle against forms of domination and oppression has certainly not disappeared—"in fact, quite the opposite!"—it is what he defines as the submission to subjectivity itself (that is, under the earlier norms deployed in subjection of entire populations and individuals, such as race or sexuality) that is responsible today for producing the most intensive and multiple new forms of social resistance—*thus the site of new strategies and counterstrategies over power sine qua non*.[30] In other words, following Canguilhem's original insight, because the norm is not founded upon a principle of intelligibility in the legitimation of power (such as a juridical-legal principle of positive law), it has become a "polemical concept."[31] (As Foucault immediately adds in the earlier lecture, "perhaps we could even call it a political concept."[32]) If it is this last description of the function of a dispositif as an imaginary point of reference that gives the subject access to her own real conditions (mind, body, subjectivity), then perhaps it is here that we also discover the closest approximation to what Althusser already described in precisely the same terms as the function of "ideological interpellation." Therefore, before turning to discuss Canguilhem's critical influence on the genealogy of the concept, it may be important to pause around the notion of what is called a "function," that is, around what Althusser himself first described precisely as an "ideological conceptual apparatus"—that is, *"the category of the subject and its functioning."*[33]

"THE CATEGORY OF THE SUBJECT AND ITS FUNCTIONING"

In the well-known investigation of ideological state apparatuses (ISAs)—a little article that was universally anthologized through the 1990s—Althusser first demonstrates what he defines as "interpellation," the most efficient technique of converting all concrete individuals into subjects so that they function within the relations of production belonging to capitalist society. Here again, we find an Aristotelian determination of "function" as a practical knowledge that is similar to the process of production in technical arts or crafts (i.e., *technē*). For example, it is by means of a knowledge specific to the carpenter that wood is converted into a chair through the application of *technē* to the material of the wood. It is this sense of *technē* as a function that Althusser will apply both to the process of production, in the material and economic sense, and to the "reproduction" of subjectivity that will be defined as the primary purpose of the ISAs. Of course, Althusser will also say that apparatuses have other functions as well. For example, "the family obviously has other 'functions' than that of an ISA. It intervenes directly in the reproduction of labor power [which is why it must be controlled]. In different modes of production, it is the unit of production and/or the unit of consumption."[34]

What is important to highlight in Althusser's investigation of the nature of this *technē* is the manner in which this function appears spontaneously as an automatic agency, that is to say, in the manner of a machine or a mechanism. This is because the product or effect of the function is already given in the beginning of the process, which, as Althusser says, is the category of the Subject itself. However, this is the same problem pertaining to an Aristotelian concept of *technē,* which is that the process is judged only by its effect; there must already be posited at the beginning an idea of "the subject and its functioning" for the reproduction of the subject to take place, just as there must be an idea of the chair before the carpenter makes an actual chair. Although this would appear to imply that the idea of a Subject exists beforehand as a "model," in the Platonic sense, this is not exactly the case, since the Subject itself does not appear as an idea of representation but rather as the very condition of the actualization of the idea of "person" or "self" in concrete individuals.

Following this understanding of the "idea," we should ask how the function of interpellation is understood to work in the manner of a machine, that is to say, in a categorical manner. This addresses a historical question: at what point did the notion of a category begin to function automatically or according to a mechanistic analogy? The answer to this question cannot be found in Althusser, who seems to accept this mechanistic understanding of category as a natural consequence of the historical development of the capitalist mode of production (i.e., the expression of a universal structure that "has no history").[35] In response, I will pose two questions: First, what is a category? Second, when does the category of the subject get invented historically to function automatically, in the manner of a machine or an apparatus (e.g., becoming the basis for understanding the function of the subject in linguistic enunciation according to Structuralism)? In other words, when did the functioning of the category naturally acquire a mechanistic attribute or become associated with the functioning of a certain kind of machine? In reply to the first question, we must briefly turn to Kant's definition of the category and its functioning. In reply to the second question, I will return to Canguilhem's essay on "Machine and Organism."

Of course, everyone knows, categories do not fall from the sky readymade. Therefore, at some point, historically, the idea of the subject had to assume a categorical function in the first place, which gives it a new determination as a concept of philosophy. Rather, the mechanistic determination of the category was invented at a particular time and place and was given this function. This occurs specifically in Kant's innovative use of the concept drawn from Aristotle. Kant asked what the automatic functioning of a category means, except that it refers to the a priori nature of the concept? A priori, in the first place, means independent of experience, that which does not depend on any a posteriori representation that is given or apprehended in experience. In effect, what Althusser is arguing is that the idea of the subject functions as a category in the Kantian sense, meaning that it is a priori and not synthetic or dependent on experience but rather a necessary and universal condition of possible experience of all concrete subjects (or individuals), particularly since he will further define all sensuous experience as already conditioned by the category of the "Subject of Ideology." It is this a priori nature in all the examples that Althusser offers to illustrate its functioning, but especially in the discovery that "individuals are always-already subjects"; moreover, "that an individual is always-already a subject, even before he is born, is the plain reality, accessible to everyone and not at all a paradox."[36]

To illustrate the last statement, I will quote the following passage from Althusser's famous essay on the "elementary ideological effect" of the categorical determination of the subject:

> As St. Paul admirably put it, it is in the "Logos," meaning in ideology, that we "live, move and have our being." It follows that, for you and for me, the category of the subject is a primary "obviousness" (obviousnesses are always primary): it is clear that you and I are subjects (free, ethical, etc. . . .). Like all obviousnesses, including those that make a word "name a thing" or "have a meaning" (therefore including the obviousness of the "transparency" of language), the "obviousness" that you and I are subjects—and that that does not cause any problems—is an ideological effect, the elementary ideological effect. It is indeed a peculiarity of ideology that it imposes (without appearing to do so, since these are "obviousnesses") *obviousnesses as obviousnesses,* which we cannot fail to recognize and before which we have the inevitable and natural reaction of crying out (aloud or in the "still, small voice of conscience"): "That's obvious! That's right! That's true!"[37]

In the preceding passage, I would simply point out the great pains that Althusser takes always to demonstrate the category of the subject, in the most concrete and practical terms, as being a priori logical, necessary, and thus already self-evident—*a fact!* What is called "a fact" expresses the immediacy of the relation between concept and predicate, which has the effect of "including the predicate"; therefore the subject is defined as an a priori analytic judgment, every individual qua individual, already contains or expresses the subject as a predicate. Phrased differently, in the manner of Althusser, there is no individual that is not already a subject, even prior to birth! At the same time, it is this "obviousness as obviousness" that Althusser will call precisely an "elementary ideological effect." In other words, the subjective feeling of the obviousness as obvious to everyone is nothing but the effect of ideology operating already through the category of the subject and its functioning.

For Althusser, "obviousness" adequately expresses the ideological meaning of an a priori category. As far as the other examples that Althusser provides for the category of the subject, they only further demonstrate that the category is obvious, that its functioning is spontaneous, self-evident, immediate, universal, and thus necessary to all possible experience by concrete subjects. In other words, the meaning of the subject is already conditioned by the a priori category of the Subject, whether we want to determine this according to Lacan's theory of the master signifier or as a "transcendental subject," according to Kant; nevertheless, both definitions define the category according to its immediate function, which requires no further demonstration or a posteriori synthesis.

In effect, Kant redefines the term *transcendental* to represent the dimension of universality that must be ascribed to the category of the Subject and its functioning as the condition for the possible experience for all concrete (i.e., empirical) individuals. As Deleuze explains in his 1978 seminar on the Kantian category:

> the formal conditions of all *apparition* must be determined as the dimensions of a subject which conditions the appearing of the *apparition* to an empirical self, this subject cannot itself be an empirical self, it will be a universal and necessary self. It's for this subject that Kant feels the need to forge or to extend a word which only had a very restrained theological use till then, thus the need to invent the notion of the transcendental, the transcendental subject being the instance which the conditions of all apparition are related to, while the *apparition* itself appears only to empirical subjects.[38]

If only to further illustrate the automatic character of spontaneity that now determines the function of the categories, I will quote another passage from the same seminar, in which Deleuze explains the birth of the transcendental subject in Kantian philosophy as the transformation of the Aristotelian concept of the category by defining it precisely in terms of a modern machine. Deleuze exclaims:

> There is indeed a subject, Kant will say, which is subordinated to appearances and which falls into sensory illusions; it will be called the empirical subject. But there is also another subject which is evidently neither you nor me, and which above all is not reducible to any empirical subject, which will be from that point onward named the transcendental subject for it is the unity of all the conditions under which something appears, appears to whom? Appears to each empirical subject. It's al-

ready beautiful as a system of ideas. I hope you can feel its extent, *it's a tremendous machine!*[39]

At this point, however, we must pause and ask the following questions: What about the a priori nature of space and time? What does Althusser do with these a priori conditions? Although I cannot go into great detail in returning to Kant's distinction between categories and the general a priori conditions of space and time, we know that Kant made a distinction between the forms of space and time and the function of categories (e.g., causality, unity, multiplicity), which are still concepts even though they do not function analytically. Space and time, according to Kant's definition, are the pure forms of our receptivity, while the concept is the form of our spontaneity or pure activity. Yet, as I have already demonstrated, Althusser gives the subject a categorical form of spontaneity or activity, so the question concerns the a priori form of time and space as "forms of receptivity." Here I will simply say that he reduces these a priori forms to being imaginary or ideological presentations—and more accurately, to employ Deleuze's word, *apparitions,* pure and simple. This distinction will play a major role in his reduction of the conditions of time and space to the status of dreams in the major statement that ideology has no history and thus is comparable to the Freudian notion of the Unconscious. In other words, ideology assumes the a priori form of receptivity for all subjects, which is to say it is an imaginary form of *apparition* that mediates all possible experience in space and time, both internal and external, to the subjects who are determined as concrete individuals. It is for this reason, finally, that we can now understand why Althusser claims that "Ideology has no history," since the "Subject of Ideology" has already internalized the forms of space and time and is not dependent or subordinated to another perspective that would be external to this categorical and immediate function, which conditions the appearance of ideology as "omnipresent, trans-historical, and immutable in form throughout the extent of history."[40] As Althusser concludes, "Ideology is eternal, exactly like the unconscious."[41]

Yet, perhaps this last statement is too *totalizing,* because it makes all relations both homogeneous and internal to the form of Ideology, as if they were both cogs in a giant machine. Here let us keep clearly in view the overall trajectory and purpose of the entirety of Althusser's argument: that the category of the subject is invented at the same moment when the forms of time and space are subordinated to the function of ideological representation of the conditions of real experience. It is on the basis of proving the invention, even the "production," of an idea of a subject who has a spontaneous and independent activity—which exists necessarily as the condition of every concrete individual—that Althusser will explain how these concrete subjects also express this tendency to work autonomously. Subjects are like little machines, which is to say, they tend to function by selling their own labor power without the need of a prime mover or a boss. According to bourgeois philosophy, all concrete subjects express this capacity simply because they choose to work, and this choice represents their elective freedom and autonomy as subjective forms of interest, even though the real conditions of an experience of extortion are removed from consciousness (i.e., the real character of slavery). From a Marxist perspective, this is merely an ideological function of disguising the conditions of real existence in an imaginary form (e.g., freedom = slavery), which is why freedom and individual liberty become the most important concepts of bourgeois philosophy following the seventeenth century; although another way of phrasing this, in the manner of Foucault, would be to say that the bourgeois society *invented* the category of the subject sometime in the middle of the seventeenth century!

At this point, we might perceive a certain convergence between Althusser and Foucault on the precise meaning of the scientific revolution, which is that both agree it is what gives birth to a bourgeois notion of the subject as a Universal Category. Specifically, what bourgeois society invents is the category of the subject as an a priori, self-evident principle of identity belonging to all concrete individuals from this point onward. Does this mean the same thing as the statement made by Foucault in the conclusion of *The Order of Things*: before the seventeenth century, "Man" does not exist? Not quite. What does Althusser say? He says that "there is no ideology except for concrete subjects, and this destination is only made possible by the subject, meaning 'by the category of the subject and its functioning.'"[42] Consequently, the form of ideology and the category of the subject are born in the same moment, and moreover, *this moment has been eternal from that point onward and includes every other moment in time, both past and future!* There is no ideology without the category of the subject, and it is the function of ideology that this category is reproduced for all concrete individuals who, naturally and spontaneously, go to work; that is to say, they function automatically, in the manner of little machines, as subjects of labor.

At the same time, it is here we come upon the most striking observation: ISAs are described precisely as machines that are reproductive, as machines that create other machines or reproduce the parts that compose still other machines. To evoke the commonplace argument on the difference between organic and mechanical forms of life, ISAs are like watches that make other watches under the principle of reproduction. ISAs are machines that imitate living biological machines, since their primary function is the reproduction of the conditions of labor. Therefore, as the effective principle of their own creation, they have, from that point onward, the idea of working independently as a definition of their purpose. In other words, it is here we find the real basis for the concept of the "Machine" in Marx and "Structure" in Althusser (i.e., the parts must be made homogenous— they must be composed of the same material and formal cause).

If Descartes is closer to Aristotle than to Plato, then in turn, Althusser is closer to Plato. Why? Because he insists on the category of the Subject as a principle given prior to its functioning in the reproduction of new concrete subjects. It exists precisely as a model in the Platonic sense, and thus all ideological representation functions unconsciously by transposing the "idea" into concrete individuals as the real subject of their functioning. In other words, if Althusser reintroduces the idea of a central Subject to which all other subjects refer in their functioning as subjects, it was only to correct a latent defect in the Cartesian theory of the subject as a spontaneous and natural category identical with God, in which God is only the principle of an efficient cause that bourgeois society invented. On the contrary, what bourgeois society invents is "the Subject and its functioning" as part of a general overall strategy whose goal, according to Althusser, is "to convert all concrete individuals into subjects of Bourgeois Ideology."[43] Of course, historically speaking, the problem is that Bourgeois Ideology ultimately failed to convert all concrete individuals into subjects, partly because what is called "power" is not a "machine"; it is not a "structure." Therefore the problem with Althusser's concept of apparatus is that he has to resort to a reproduction of the term itself to define its order, or primary axiomatic function. In other words, the apparatus is already determined as part of a more general order to which its function is subordinated, the capitalist mode of production. Once again, this leads to a tautology in the category itself, which he can resolve only by describing certain state apparatuses as repressive, directly subjecting the body to power or force (the police, the prison, the military), and others defined as ideological, whose form of subjection is imaginary, producing in the consciousness a correlate of the subjected body in the form of an identity, which Foucault refers to later as a kind of "autonomous docility."

For Foucault, on the other hand (as well as for Canguilhem, as we will see in the next section), the emphasis is placed not on the category of the Subject but rather on the *disposability* of the parts or elements in a spatial and temporal unity. Different elements are so arranged in space and time that their unity and their identity are expressed, not as analytic predicates of the same subject, but as synthetic predicates of the whole arrangement or order (discursive, social, military, penal, or disciplinary). Therefore, somewhat similar to the implicit criticism of standardization that is the basic principle of a Marxist economic theory of capitalization (i.e., the calculation of prices by labor time), it is rather the development of mechanization itself that is "the authentic cause of the mechanization of the universe."[44] At this point, Foucault's theory of the distinction between "apparatus" (*appareil*) and "dispositif" (*dispositif*) is derived from Canguilhem, who, as we will see, finds it first in Descartes, and not in Marx. Likewise, for Foucault, a new demand appears to which disciplinary society must respond, that is, to construct a living machine, an entire organism, whose effect will be maximized by the concerted articulation of the elementary parts of which it is composed. Discipline is no longer simply an art of distributing bodies, of extracting time from them and accumulating it, "but of composing forces in order to obtain a much more efficient machine."[45]

THE BIRTH OF THE CARTESIAN DISPOSITIF

Let us now turn to the second question: "historically speaking, exactly when did the functioning of the subject of power acquire this mechanistic analogy"? Although Althusser's argument is also that the liberal subject was essentially a bourgeois invention, that is to say, an invented and artificial subject whose functioning can be described in terms of an apparatus or machine, we will find a more historical explanation at the core of Canguilhem's earlier discussion of "machine and organism."[46] Ultimately, Canguilhem would not disagree with Althusser's proposition that bourgeois society "invented" the category of the subject of "autonomous freedom" or that this understanding of function was predicated on a transformation of the idea of the mechanism in modern machines. (In fact, that is also the central thesis of Canguilhem's argument in "Machine and Organism," written twenty years before Althusser's notes on the "Ideological State Apparatus.") Rather, it is simply that this process of technological evolution did not take place through a change in the philosophical regime of representation itself, which only occurred retroactively (a thesis perhaps more in keeping with Heidegger's criticism of Cartesianism as the representational order of modern technology), but instead through a gradual process of mechanization of various material and technical practices, and especially with the invention of new political dispositifs, which is more in keeping with Foucault's description from *Discipline and Punish* onward.

In Canguilhem's earlier essay on "Machine and Organism," we have the first known usage of the term *dispositif* to denote simply the idea of mechanism applied in modern biology. According to this definition, Canguilhem writes, "With the exception of vertebrates, living beings and their forms rarely display to the scrupulous observer devices [*dispositifs*] that could evoke the idea of a mechanism, in the sense given to this term by scientists."[47] Moreover, the second definition that Canguilhem gives to the term is simply that of a tool that is invented or fabricated to act on nature, as described by modern ethnographers, but also he points out that the rationalization of techniques to explain the invention of specific tools (or machines) seems "to forget the irrational origin of machines themselves."[48] This leads to a crucial point that I already introduced: it is the innate tendency to rationalize the idea of mechanism, as Descartes did, as a knowledge that is particular to the subject of Man and not a universal biological phenomenon that is already found to be latent in all organisms, which anthropomorphizes the natural relation between machine and organism in the form of a rupture or discontinuity that the form of rationalization of the idea of mechanism in modern science first introduces. In fact, as Canguilhem demonstrates many times in this brief article, it is the construction of machines that is actually chronologically anterior to any technical knowledge that seeks to appropriate the machine (tool) to inform its certain specific ends or to multiply its effects (including its powers over living beings), because "every technique essentially and positively includes a vital originality irreducible to rationalization."[49] Consequently, for Canguilhem, the image of vital originality might be better illustrated by the partly irrational origins of some of the machines invented by Leonardo da Vinci, which Freud recounts in his psychoanalytic study, than by Descartes's image of God as the watchmaker, where we find the idea of mechanism already completely rationalized according to a seventeenth-century understanding of mechanism. Canguilhem's image of this "vital originality" echoes, intentionally perhaps, Heidegger's question concerning the origin of the work of art that appears in Germany two years beforehand. As I will argue concerning Foucault's adaptation of Canguilhem's earlier observation to his understanding of the techniques of power and sexuality, just as the construction of certain machines is before the knowledge of techniques that employ them, the invention of dispositifs is prior to knowledge of the effect or final cause (i.e., analytical representation), and thus in some ways can be compared to the knowledge responsible for the creation of works of art, which cannot be completely rationalized beforehand. A much simpler way of putting this is that the idea of mechanism is based on the construction of actual machines, and not the other way around; the knowledge employed in the construction of machines is not the same as the form of rationalization that is applied to this vital originality later on, whether this concerns the work of art or the tool of technology.

To prove this thesis, Canguilhem acknowledges that both Marx and Borkenau claimed that the "mechanistic view of the universe" was a fundamentally bourgeois *Weltanschauung*; however, he also observes that difference between these claims is a hundred years apart, and more importantly, nearly eighty years before La Mettrie's *Man a Machine,* at which point we can say that this worldview is fully consolidated in the fields of both philosophy and biology. Contrary to both claims, therefore, Canguilhem actually locates the first sign of its emergence in Descartes's 1662 *Treatise of Man,* but, most importantly, in da Vinci's diagrams and compositions of humans, animals, and various *machina.* On this point, he follows Henry Grossman's earlier criticism of Borkenau: that he skips over 150 years of economic and ideological history by seeking to locate the mechanistic conception as contemporaneous with the stage of industrial manufacturing, "as if Leonardo DaVinci never existed!"[50] In other words, by the time of Marx, this mechanistic view of the "subject and its functioning" was already completely "naturalized" (as I have already argued), and thus a Cartesian mechanical understanding already informed Marx's representation of the functioning of the state as a particular kind of machine in the "Early Works" (1841–44).

The only question that Marx will raise in 1844 is what kind of machine the modern state represents. In the answer he first provides to this question, it is crucial to observe that Marx also criticizes and eventually rejects the classical analogies mechanism and organism in favor of a distinctly modern machine: the steam engine. Consequently, in the section of volume 1 of *Das Kapital,* on the question of surplus value, Marx gives us an indication of the special machine he has in mind by quoting the following definition from Charles Babbage: "a machine is formed by the reunion of all these simple instruments that are placed in motion by a unique motor."[51] In other words, it is precisely at this moment that Marx understands the special nature of a distinctly modern machine, opposed to the classical mechanical apparatus of Descartes and La Mettrie, by the uniqueness of the motor function that causes all the components to move together, and by the nature of the force that causes movement. For example, Marx writes, "the infant has his own force of movement just as the steam engine," and the function of the motor that is special to each kind of machine is described as the transformation of one kind of energy into another (for example, caloric energy into kinetic energy).[52]

Ultimately, it is by means of this thermodynamic analogy that Marx is able to determine the "special machine" of the state by the uniqueness of its motor from which it derives its energy to function. The law is a force that functions as the motor of the state, and all individuals recognize it as a special kind of machine that appears from "outside" the space of civil society and functions automatically powered by a "miraculous" power: the machine derives its energy by converting raw class inequality into legal violence, by which the state first appears to separate itself from civil society, only to more effectively intervene into the corporate life of the community, including the life of the family, and to enforce its own form of universal Right. It is only in this way that we can understand how the reproduction of class inequality, even the production of new forms of inequality, provides the motor of the state-machine with the energy it needs to function, even though it is made to appear that the state exists to end these forms of inequality.

This function is nothing less than the function of Ideology *tout court*! Simply put, new forms of inequality provide the state-machine with the energy it requires to function and to expand across all social relations in order to convert concrete individuals into ideological subjects through the process of subjection proper. (It can even be said to drill into all relations of inequality to discover new sources of the energy it demands to function in the role of a liberator!) Finally, this transformation of energy is actually responsible for the fabrication of the special body of the state and its functionaries into an apparatus (composed of the police, the military, the bureaucrats, the corporation), because the very *mettle* of their bodies, the material from which they are composed, is suddenly transformed into a unified and special matter in the same way that the bodies of soldiers in a platoon have the consistency of one kind of metal or bureaucrats in a vast office in Kafka's *Castle* can be said all to be materially made from the same cloth. This will also become the basis for Althusser's later claim that all concrete subjects are composed of the same signifying matter, which is to say, *they are all identical in their Subject*! This identification gives them not only biological life *(bios)* but also spiritual life (soul, or ψυχή), which is subtracted from both animals and plants. As we have already seen, this occurs in Descartes and not in Aristotle; at this point, anthropologically speaking, human animals become biological machines that are also endowed with the category of the Subject that was placed into them by God.

According to Canguilhem's central argument, this introduces a new species of anthropocentrism at the end of the seventeenth century: "Descartes' project of explaining life mechanically eliminates purpose in its anthropomorphic form. Yet in realizing this project, one anthropomorphism is merely substituted for an earlier one—a technological anthropomorphism is substituted for a political anthropomorphism."[53] Perhaps a more modern and technologically accurate manner of saying this is that a "command function" (as in cybernetic theory) is substituted for the political image of commandment that previously belonged to a now archaic and theological image of sovereign power. Therefore, according to Canguilhem, "while it may be said that, in substituting mechanism for the organism, Descartes effaces teleology from life, but he does so only in appearance, for he reassembles it, in its entirety, as his point of departure."[54] In other words, Descartes inscribed the modern idea mechanism within an already preexisting model of the compound *animal-machine-sovereign*; that is to say, he consciously rationalized the vital notion of life itself in his understanding of God as the principle of the New Science.

This anthropomorphizing of the animal-machine-sovereign complex is perhaps Canguilhem's most radical critique of the "Cartesian dispositif"—and I am using the term intentionally—a critique that is contained in three steps, which I have already outlined above but will restate against the backdrop of our discussion of Althusser:

(a) First, if God is both the efficient and final cause of the mechanism of life, then he already contains infinite knowledge concerning the evolutionary path of future mechanisms, and one need only refer to this principle in rectifying the most current mechanistic understanding with the mind of God, who functions as its first principle. In other words, Descartes first institutes the idea of mechanism in the idea of God, in the same way that Marx institutes the updated idea of mechanism in the state, and finally, in the way that Althusser institutes the most current definition of mechanism in the categorical function of the Subject, which is to say, the function of a structure without a central subject of sovereignty. In some ways, this procedure functions no differently than updating the software of the central subject according to the idea of its function to function categorically for all other elements.

(b) Second, this leads to Canguilhem's most trenchant and severe criticism of the technological understanding of "organic life," which reintroduces a fundamental dehiscence between technological machines (apparatuses) and living machines (bodies), on the presumption that only the former require efficient causes (since machines do not create other machines). In some ways, this reintroduces a functional lack into the machinic phylum, almost in the same manner that Foucault describes the dispositif of sexuality introducing anatomical lack into the body of women (and the gradual recovery of this missing organ of "life" has been a constant narrative thread of posthuman theories and science fiction as well).

(c) Third, and finally, in the history of science, the epistemology of technology is never given once and for all, and thus the hybrid concepts of organism and machine cannot be established through a historical understanding of technique, nor on the basis of the most recent image of technology. This will also lead to Foucault's basic insight that the dispositif belongs to an order of technique that is patently artificial, requiring constant reinvention, adaptation, correction, and new techniques and tactics, but it is also vulnerable to sudden reversals, appropriation, and counterstrategy by power relations. Thus, like the process that defines living itself through the encounter with the environment in an agonistic struggle to maintain equilibrium, the evolutionary path of any technological dispositif is equally open to the chance of radical error concerning its own finality (e.g., the atomic bomb, the computer, the internet, the robot or cyborg, artificial intelligence).

Concluding our discussion of the birth of the "Cartesian dispositif," Descartes consciously rationalized a mechanistic technique rather than unconsciously translating the practices of a nascent capitalist economy, as many have argued. "Consequently," as Canguilhem concludes, "we say that Descartes integrated into his philosophy a human phenomenon—the construction of machines—much more than he transposed into ideology the social phenomenon of capitalist production."[55] Therefore, if the category of the *cogito* specifically invented by Descartes is generally regarded as the hallmark of modern philosophy, this occurs by conscious rationalization of the animal-machine and not by unconscious transposition of an early capitalist mode of production into the order of philosophical representation. Although this might appear to some as an argument on the head of a pin, as we have already seen, it will become a crucial one for Foucault, who often talks in his later interviews about not wanting to rationalize power by providing a general theory based on an already given understanding of an apparatus or an economic, materialist explanation of power relations, because by describing power this way, one might be superimposing an outdated model of "administrative monarchy," with its "machinery of control," on the contemporary field of real power relations.[56] In fact, his maxim not to rationalize power as well the accompanying maxim "never make a politics in theory" *(ne faire jamais de politique)* may both refer to an early insight that he had gained from Canguilhem's critique of Descartes.[57] Both maxims can be summarized as epistemological rules of research in avoiding the trap of an implicit teleology in describing the evolution of techniques and the invention of new dispositifs of power and governmentality by recourse to earlier mechanisms of political economy, as we will see in the next section, concerning the genealogy of the "biopolitical dispositif."

3. Grid of Intelligibility

From the relatively short period of a few years following the publication of the first volume of *The History of Sexuality* and the lecture course on *Security, Territory, Population* of 1977–78, there is a parallel thesis established between the evolution of disciplinary and security techniques directed at the level of populations or species and the evolution of the concept of freedom that is first established at the level of the individual under the classical doctrine of liberalism, but which gradually becomes identified with the multiple and micrological processes of life itself. As Foucault emphasizes, "freedom is nothing else but the correlative deployment of the apparatuses of security."[1] In other words, there is a very tight correlation of biopolitical security apparatuses (i.e., health, sexuality, deviancy, hygiene, etc.) with the forces of contingency, discontinuity, economy, and circulation that will come to the forefront of the 1978–79 lectures that compose the so-called *Birth of Biopolitics.*[2]

Foucault employs this new model as a lever to pry the analysis of power away from a classical mechanistic and modern Structuralist determination of agency; hence, the subject of power no longer exclusively refers to a positive and heterogeneous agency of the law, or to a sovereign figure, but rather functions as a "normative autonomous agent."[3] Nevertheless, here we should be cautious in merely substituting one analogy for another, a biological one for a mechanical one, or even in producing an ontological version of "biopower" that is primarily metaphorical. Here we can see why there have been so many misinterpretations of Foucault precisely around the term *biopower*, because these readings have often assumed that power no longer functions or occurs through its disciplinary mechanisms (e.g., the Panoptic mechanism) but has been replaced wholesale by a powerful new paradigm that simply operates according to another analogy, the organism, and by means of a different kind of energy, biological energy (i.e., *bios*).

To illustrate this epistemological problem, let us now return to the earlier statement from the 1975 lectures on the abnormal, which marks the first instance where Foucault introduces his "pivotal distinction."[4] What does he say exactly? He says that this year, instead of the mechanics of the disciplinary apparatus, he will be looking at the "effects of normalization," which are defined as the effective function of various new dispositifs of security. This statement does not imply that organism replaces mechanism, that biopower replaces discipline, but that both coexist in a total social organization and operate according to different principles that both separate them and, at the same time, unify them in a "typical form of governmentality." In other words, biopolitical dispositifs are simply the other side of juridical and political structures of representation and even serve as the condition of their functioning and effectiveness. For example, if the technique of subjection functions much more effectively today as "a mode of subjectivation" *(mode de assujuttissment)*, by which concrete individuals are actually transformed into neoliberal subjects, the biopolitical dispositif becomes "typical," "ordinary," and "common," as a power that everyone in the social field possesses and is possessed by, recalling the famous line from Auden where one cannot tell the difference between the dancer and the dance. Once again, we see Foucault's favorite pair of conceptual terms for the conditions of emergence of historical dispositifs, *dispersion and generality, rather than totalization and universality!*

This brings us to Foucault's initial discussions of neoliberalism when Foucault first addresses the concept of "biopolitics" explicitly in relation to what he accounts for as the influence of some of the principles of German ordoliberalism during the postwar period, but primarily from the influence on national economic policies of Great Britain and the United States by members of the Mont Pèlerin Society (Hayek, Friedman, Stigler, Popper, Polanyi, Einaudi).[5] However, it is important to point out in the 1979 seminars beginning in January that, while Foucault promises a complete picture of the different national and economic arrangements that result from what he identified as the "dispersion" of the German ordoliberal model, including the hybrid form that neoliberalism assumes in American society through the influence of the Chicago School that was taking place also at precisely this moment, he eventually restricts his analysis mostly to the key figures of the earlier Freiburg School, and especially those aspects that are consistent with his earlier work on disciplinary society, especially the analysis of criminality and juvenile delinquency.[6] This is clearly announced in the March 7, 1979, lecture: "I would have liked to assure you that, in spite of everything, I really did intend to talk about biopolitics, and then, things being what they are, I have ended up talking at length, and maybe too long, about neoliberalism and neoliberalism in its German form."

In the 1978–79 lectures, moreover, many of Foucault's own examples of biopolitics concern the growth of new techniques in measuring the birthrate in national populations, child-rearing in the family, and juvenile delinquency in civil society, to which we might also add several other values of "human capital" (e.g., education, hygiene, mental health). In other words, this constitutes the program of what is generally identified with the so-called economization of the private sphere of society, which became the hallmark of what ordoliberal economist Wilhelm Röpke called *Gesellschaftspolitik* and Alexandre von Rüstow called *Vitalpolitik*. What Foucault will conclude from these policies is the extension of new techniques of governing living bodies and populations (including other species), techniques and their corresponding knowledges that "cross the threshold of the traditional political sciences" and extend the problem of governmentality "beyond its former limits, including all the spheres of life in the government's political activity," including, I might add, the life of other species and "non-human animals within the bio political frame."[7]

As Foucault quotes from Bilger's *La Pensée économique liberale de L'Allemagne contemporaine* (1966), upon which he relies for much of his own understanding of German ordoliberal theory, "Rüstow defined *Vitalpolitik* [as] a policy of life, which is not essentially orientated to increased earnings and reduced hours for the worker, like traditional social policy of labor time, but which takes cognizance of the worker's whole vital situation, his real, concrete situation, from morning to night and from night to

morning" (including material and moral hygiene, sense of property and social integration, etc.).[8] In other words, the major problem posed by postwar
German ordoliberalist theories was how to redefine a market society made
up from purely "raw" or "cold" values (i.e., the principle of unrestrained
economic competition) without this principle itself causing the fabric of
civil society to unravel. As Röpke said, "competition is a principle of order
in the domain of the market economy, but it is not a principle on which
it would be possible to erect the whole of society."[9] This would become a
major point of contention and eventual divergence of neoliberal doctrine
with Hayek, and later on with members of the Chicago School (e.g., Friedman, Becker, Schultz), who argued that liberal society can only function
when all the individual elements, which function like variables, accept the
principle of economic order as a kind of "reality principle."[10]

In large part, this represents a fundamental dispute over the classical
liberal principles of free market economy, often leading to a laissez-faire
state that in some ways resembles a Hobbesian state of nature. Rüstow, who,
along with Erhard and Röpke, is considered one of the primary economic
theorists of "social market theory," proposed to resolve this ambiguity in
the following manner: "since competition is a principle that dissolves more
than it unifies, we have to organize the economy of the social body according to the rules of the market economy, but at the same time, to infuse these
principles with a number of affirmative values to buffer the individual from
the disintegrating and atomistic effects of pure, raw, or cold competition."[11]
These principles of the German *Gesellschaftpolitik* were largely responsible
for the post-1948 "economic miracle," that is, the generalization of the entire social field under the extended principles of enterprise and competition, but at the same time, the regulation of competition according to a
set of "warm," "light" political and moral values that are created to offset
the "cold" and strictly calculating measures of unrestrained economic competition over the production of human capital that spreads into formerly
nonpoliticized spheres of society. For example, here is a quote from a 1963
feature article in *Life* magazine concerning the German economic miracle:

> Today the German working-man leads a comfortable life and wears a
> well-filled waistcoat. He eats well, and his food—although German
> cooking lacks the elegance of French—is wholesome and appetizing.
> He buys good clothes, and he dresses his wife and children well. He gen-

erally has money to spare for television sets, week-end excursions and football matches. And he is not afraid of celebrating occasionally on a grander scale.[12]

Likewise, under Rüstow, the primary concern of *Vitalpolitik* was in shaping the subjective forms of human capital in its most individuated expressions, that is to say, to normalize processes of subjectification in order that subjects be integrated into the free market society without overt coercion or the potentially disintegrating reaction caused by power's overt manifestation as a violent, dominating, or repressive force. These positive values of "affirmative biopolitics" can be understood as corollaries to Foucault's basic thesis concerning the goals of biopolitical dispositifs that enhance the productive forces of life (i.e., a government of the living) and will serve to supplement—and, in some areas, to mitigate, especially in advanced capitalist societies—the coercive presence of sovereign violence (i.e., the government of death).

In reference to both Rüstow's argument concerning a positive *Vitalpolitik* and Foucault's own analysis of the growth of nineteenth-century *Poliziewissenschafften* (i.e., "police sciences," taken in its broadest sense, including the laws of commerce and circulation) that forms the basis of his own investigation into the new economic "grid of intelligibility," it is crucial to see that these new knowledges or techniques are not immediately assumed already to function as official mechanisms of administrative control (e.g., ISAs) but rather to constitute an unformed array of new knowledges and techniques that emerged around the same time as the new neoliberal art of governmentality. (For example, Foucault's evidence amounts to the sheer explosion of bibliographic entries over a twenty-year period at the end of the eighteenth century.) For Rüstow, the knowledges that constitute the special region of the social policies of *Vitalpolitik*—again, "a policy for enhancing the quality of life"—mostly stem from what he often refers to as the "new anthropology," which, in the 1950s, corresponded with the emergence of sociology as an official academic discipline in Western universities. As for Foucault, this area of research foregrounds his interest in tracking the emergence of new disciplinary knowledges in the social sciences, and especially the statistical arts, which are gradually incorporated into what he calls the "neoliberal art of government."[13] Accordingly, these new knowledges and techniques, which will ultimately compose the biopolitical grid of intelligibility, can be understood as expressions of "a new political economy," the overall strategy of which is not the takeover (*étatisation*) of society so much as the "governmentalization" of the state.[14]

Moreover, under the term *diffusion*, Foucault also traces in the history of American liberalism the "diffusion" of some (though not all) of the principles of *Gesellschaftpolitik*. At the same time, he remarks on the problem or the ambiguity that is inherent in the principles that American society has adopted, which differentiate its path into contemporary neoliberalist polity from that of Germany and France, including a different social character in the investment of human capital as well as the historical antinomy of the state and civil society in European societies. Thus many of the cold values of individual competition are indeed made light and warm (i.e., subjective, choice based, or consumerist), even though they continue to promote unrestrained and generalized forms of competition between groups, classes, and races. In addition, the American path into neoliberalism has the tendency to engender new forms of competition throughout the social body (e.g., "identity politics"), although, in this case, the principle of competition itself blends into the general fabric of society so that one can no longer see the difference between the economic principle of competition and the individual or collective principle of liberty being expressed as a form of social interest. To quote from Foucault's 1978 seminar:

> on one side it means generalizing the "enterprise" form within the social body or social fabric [for example, as we have been witnessing for some time in universities under the principle of "corporatization"]; it means taking this fabric and arranging things so that it can be broken down, subdivided, and reduced, not according to the grain of individuals, but according to the grain of [private] enterprises. The individual's life must be lodged, not within the framework of a big enterprise or firm, or, if it comes to it, the state, but within the framework of a multiplicity of diverse enterprises connected up and entangled with other enterprises that are in some way ready to hand for the individual, sufficiently limited in their scale for the individual's actions, decisions, and choices to have meaningful and perceptible effects and numerous enough for him not to be dependent on one alone. And finally, the individual's life itself—with his relationships to private property, for example, with his family, household, insurance, and retirement—must make him into a sort of permanent and multiple enterprise.[15]

In this passage, what Foucault is first calling our attention to is the emergence of neoliberal policies as well new juridical mechanisms that actually seek to restrict the power of the state to intervene directly into the affairs of economic life—and most critically in the areas of collective security, property, and the protection of individual freedoms (e.g., the pursuit of happiness, the right to subjectivity). In fact, it is around this set of economic-ethical ambiguities that Foucault defines a later evolution of the general theory of biopolitics, which amounts to the generalization of a notion of "enterprise" throughout every part of the social fabric.[16] As I will return to discussing later, it is crucial to observe that what Foucault is describing as the principles of the German model of *Vitalpolitik* Gilles Deleuze will twelve years later define as principles of "a Society of Control."

At the same time, it is important to point out that while Foucault first sets out to examine the emergence of this new political economy in contemporary neoliberal society, by the midpoint of the year, he restricts his analysis to the earliest incarnations mostly drawn from the proceedings that took place in the Walter Lippmann Colloquium on the eve of the war in 1939.[17] This is clearly announced in the lecture of March 7, 1979: "I would have liked to assure you that, in spite of everything, I really did intend to talk about biopolitics, and then, things being what they are, I have ended up talking at length, and maybe too long, about neo-liberalism and neo-liberalism in its German form."[18] Foucault places greater emphasis on the analysis of the German model of ordoliberalism, given that he finds an echo of the same problem that is proposed around his thesis of *homo economicus*: from the beginning of the eighteenth century onward, the question is whether it is possible to invent a technique or strategy of governmentality that replaces an earlier model of state sovereignty and, at the same time, will ultimately prove to be capable of governing interests of modern economic man. Of course, many readers have simply assumed that the answer to this question would be yes and that the strategic form of governmentality evidenced by contemporary neoliberal society (i.e., "a society of control") has effectively supplanted a need for the state-form or the old principle of sovereign power to rule the multiple forms of interest that constantly break out in neoliberal society. And yet, nothing could be further from the truth, especially since Foucault will repeatedly say no. In fact, the interests of *homo economicus* have proven themselves over the course of the past two centuries to be downright *"ungovernment-able* [*sic*]."[19]

This negative judgment and the critique of classical political economy that it proposes is the basis of Foucault's own line of inquiry, which is no longer the question "What is the best form of the state?" but rather "What is the proper role of the techniques of governmentality with regard to the conduct of *homo economicus*?" Of course, the question of technique raised here does not primarily address the role of the executive, or the sovereign, because, as Foucault concludes, the historical evidence has shown us that "there is no economic sovereign. Thus, all the returns and revivals of nineteenth and twentieth century liberal and neo-liberal thought are still a way of posing the problem of the impossibility of the existence of an economic sovereign."[20] In other words, if, beginning already in the seventeenth century, the economy is indeed "world-making" or "world-forming," as classical liberalism claims along with Smith's theory of the invisible hand, then all the degrees of human capital from alienation to the satisfaction of interest can be located there. These are the principles at the basis of what Foucault describes, following Hume and British empiricism, as a new subject beginning in the eighteenth century: *homo economicus,* in distinction from *homo juridicus,* the subject of right. The question that Foucault immediately underlines, however, is whether this new subject can be brought into coordination with the juridical subject of rights, and whether the new techniques and knowledges operated by modern states are equipped to fashion this correspondence, or whether new juridical mechanisms will need to be invented to serve this purpose. If so, then who would control these new juridical mechanisms of control: the state or the economic elites? (I think there is sufficient historical evidence to conclude that this question, raised at the end of the 1970s, has been answered mostly in favor of the latter. Nevertheless, this is the same problem that is repeatedly posed concerning the earlier versions of neoliberalism during the postwar period.) Perhaps another way of posing the same question, in more Kantian terms, is whether the economic subject motivated by self-interest can ever be brought into harmony with the subject of right, duty, and the rule of law.

From a different point of view, with the preceding observations, we see a relationship between so-called discipline and biopolitics that cannot be represented by a wholesale paradigm change, as in many contemporary discussions of biopolitics, but rather something that resembles instead the multiplication of formerly separated centers of action (political, juridical, economic, cultural, or social), all of which are mixed and interpenetrated in the contemporary period. For example, after introducing the principles of *Vitalpolitik* in the lecture of February 14, 1979, Foucault exclaims, "An enterprise society and a judicial society framed by the multiplicity of juridical institutions, are in fact two faces of a single phenomenon."[21] However, because the subject of enterprise does not quite fit together in a mechanical sense with the subject of rights, "*a new plane of reference is needed*" (according to a geometrical analogy) for situating the "complex whole" of civil society outside the apparatus of the state, also recalling our earlier discussion of the location of the "complex idea" within the earlier dispositifs of sexuality and madness. (Moreover, let us also recall that the space in which the idea first appears is a heterogeneous and yet concrete ensemble of "discourses, institutions, administrative measures, scientific statements, philosophical, moral and philanthropic propositions.")[22] In fact, at one point in his discussion of the historical emergence of "civil society" as both an idea and an element of biopolitical dispositif, Foucault invokes once again the "art of geometry" in his definition of the new grid of intelligibility that will come to determine the art of neoliberal governmentality.

If we accept that the primary form of socialization of all collective life is economic simply by virtue of the fact that while all subjects (or citizens) do not necessarily participate in the political sphere of society (whether due to repression or volunteerism), all life is included in the economy (even when certain forms of life are excluded as forms of human capital). Hayek is perhaps the strongest proponent of this viewpoint on the limitations of individual liberty, and he frequently denounces the notion of freedom as an exercise of personal participation in political decisions: "you cannot activate your species being by participation in the polis."[23] Accordingly, if politics is not permanently split between the sphere of economics, over which there is no sovereign, and the sphere of law, which can only address the subject of duties and rights, this art must be given a new compass, a new reference point, a new reality or domain on which it will be exercised, which is a new conceptual device for mapping elemental distinctions in real social space itself, distinctions that exist no longer only between individuals or groups but at a micropolitical level of the social bond itself.

Recalling what I referred to earlier as the problem of curvature that is specific to real social space, in which individuals already exist or already dwell inside strategies, one of the defining characteristics of a nineteenth-century understanding of civil society is a spontaneous and permanent matrix of power relations.[24] In other words, it is because power occurs somewhat spontaneously across the social field that power relations themselves seem to multiply and proliferate, producing new forms of inequality and concrete differences between private and public, individual and collective, subjectivities. Therefore, if today we are witnessing the multiplication of new mechanisms and social techniques to limit (and, it is hoped, to mediate) the growing number of conflicts engendered by the neoliberal principles of Enterprise, which Foucault describes as the multiplication of surfaces of friction and potential legal disputes that intersect between the private and the public spheres, then it also follows that many of these mechanisms have now expanded beyond the control of political and juridical authority. Indeed, it is for this reason that a "new plane of reference is needed" for what we call the "political" today, because many of these new mechanisms can no longer be centralized upon any state-form, nor can these new subjects of power be represented by an earlier apparatus *(appareil)* of administrative control, nor by what is now a clearly outdated theory of political economy.[25]

THE PRINCIPLE OF *VITALPOLITIK*

Let us look more closely at the primary theories of Rüstow and Röpke, the two leading ordoliberal economists who were exiled during the Nazi period, who both returned to participate in the postwar reconstruction of the German market economy. In fact, both strongly opposed classical liberal mantra of laissez-faire in the belief that the economic sphere alone was too narrow to provide a stable form of social integration for a free market society.[26] In his three-volume magnum opus published soon after returning from exile in 1945, Rüstow vindicates Rousseau's earlier pessimism concerning modernization (at the same time calling him "pathological" and prone to "emotionalism"), as well as Marx and Engel's critique of the classical economic theory of Smith and Ricardo. However, he restricts the term *capitalism* to refer only to the free market principles that were dominant throughout the nineteenth and early twentieth centuries but were exploited by powerful monopolies and political interests, including the nationalization of the economy under national socialism and Soviet communism, as well as the various formations of economic protectionism in England and the United States. Here I quote a passage from the abridged English version of the three-volume *Ortsbestimmung der Gegenwart* (1949), which, interestingly enough, was published on the eve of the rise of neoliberalism under Thatcher and Reagan in the 1980s:

> The economy of the nineteenth and twentieth centuries, called "capitalist," is a pathological degeneration. . . . We distinguish, therefore, the free-market economy of perfect competition which constitutes the normal object of liberal economic theory, from the subsidy-ridden, monopolist, protectionist, pluralist economy of the nineteenth and twentieth centuries that resulted from a quasi-theological perversion of *laissez-faire,* and it is this last we designate as "capitalist" and "capitalism."[27]

"Capitalism," in other words, is the name of a "degenerate form of market economy" that has existed from the end of the eighteenth century through the immediate prewar period.[28] In the preceding passage, moreover, we can already see the basis of utopian argument that is at the center of Rüstow's voluminous work written mostly from exile in Turkey and published immediately prior to the postwar reconstruction of the West German economy. In short, according to his argument, authentic free market economy historically never existed but was always betrayed by powerful monopolies and national state and class actors. In fact, both Röpke and Rüstow believed (as did Hayek, but for very different reasons) that what classical liberalism lacked was precisely a utopian worldview of the future, which placed it at a disadvantage with both socialist theory of economic planning and Keynesian principles of a strong interventionist and centralized state-form. Of course, the two primary credos of liberalism, neo- or not, are an aversion to centralization (whether referring the socialist state, the Nazi regime, or even the contemporary federalist democracy in the United States), as well as any strong interventionism or state planning of the economy.

In the case of Hayek, in particular, the argument turns around a theory of a strong versus weak state-form, which ironically also recalls the arguments of Schmitt (who Hayek, in fact, echoes on many occasions, although he is also careful not to directly cite him, including in his defense of the Pinochet regime in Chile).[29] For example, Hayek wrote:

> Liberalism and democracy, although compatible, are not the same. The opposite of liberalism is totalitarianism, while the opposite of democracy is authoritarianism. In consequence, it is at least possible in principle that a democratic government may be totalitarian and that an authoritarian government may act on liberal principles . . . [in] demanding unlimited power of the majority, [democracies] become essentially anti-liberal.[30]

The problem that Rüstow underlines is that there has been no state-form, either in its history or in its current geopolitical context, that has actually been "strong enough" to protect its own sphere of legitimate operation and authority from even stronger forms of interest that emerge either from within the state itself, in the case of bureaucracy, or from the "parasitic" sectors of civil society. Consequently, if the modern state is invested with the belief that its role is to guarantee equality between all social segments, then the basic tenet of neoliberalist doctrine is that this belief is unfounded, even cynical, since this ideology fails to address the actual products of state power in whatever form it has taken historically, whether in socialism, fascism, communism, or modern democracy.

Moreover, accepting that neoliberalism is not a unified and coherent *Weltanschauung* at all the stages of its development, or between the opposing schools of thought, we must not conflate the idea of a "strong" state given here by Hayek, according to a Schmittian definition, with the idea of a totalized or "weak" state as it is first defined by Rüstow; what is often identified as a "strong state" is actually "weak," according to Rüstow's analysis. As already evidenced in the passage quoted earlier, "totalization" (i.e., what Foucault will call *étatisation*) leads to a weakened state-form (as in the case of the socialism, or in the case of many modern democracies) when the state-form attempts to totalize all social relations, often leading to a kind of pluralism in which powerful political interests appropriate different segments of state power (executive, legislative, and juridical) and the "rule of the *demos*" is constantly vulnerable to the return of authoritarianism, such as the form of popular dictatorship in the United States today. In a socialist state, this can also occur when different sectors of a vast bureaucracy begin competing over the parts or sectors of the state apparatus itself, leading to economic inefficiency, as had occurred in France immediately prior to the period in which Foucault was making his own analysis of neoliberal principles that were just being introduced during the 1970s. In other words, Foucault's analysis had clearly in view the emerging principles of the neoliberal governmentality of the *post-dirigiste* context as a primary motivation for the research on the evolution of contemporary neoliberal doctrines departing from the principles of classical liberalism.

Second, recalling the definition of "capitalism" as a degenerate market society that either leads to the disintegration of individual liberties through a process Rüstow calls "superstratification" (i.e., domination of the economy by one social stratum or "economic elite") or to what Foucault himself defined as the "totalization" *(étatisation)* of society by a state-form "that moves beyond its proper limits," we should point out that, according to ordoliberal theory, unlike in the political theory of Schmitt, the state is actually ascribed a proper sphere of its own. As Rüstow writes:

> there is an almost universal view . . . that the expansion of government power beyond its former limits, this involvement of all the spheres of life in the government's political activity, is a sign of the excessive strength of the State, a sort of hubris, a matter of the State no longer knowing its limits. In truth, it is a sign of the most deplorable weakness of the State . . . which can no longer defend itself against the concerted attack of vested interests. . . . Each interest group appropriates a piece of State power and exploits it for its own ends.[31]

At this point, I will pause for a moment around the description of a form of power (or sovereignty) that extends "beyond its former limits" and ask whether this is not a perfect description of the concept of biopower (and/or biopolitics) that has been applied willy-nilly to the current neoliberal state-form by many of Foucault's readers? As I have already recounted, in reference to both Rüstow's argument concerning the principles of what he calls "a positive *Vitalpolitik*" and Foucault's analysis of the growth of nineteenth-century *Poliziewissenschafften,* most of these principles were not established by any existing state-form but emerged from the sphere of what Foucault defines as the "complex whole" of civil society according to a specifically nineteenth-century phenomenon that he compares to the emergence of the dispositifs of madness and sexuality in the exact same period. It is unfortunate that Foucault's cursory remarks on this relationship in the very last lecture of April 1979 were never explored in any systematic manner—*neither by Foucault himself in the subsequent five years nor by any of his closest readers since his death in 1984!*

Of course, Foucault's observation does not mean that the concept of "civil society" didn't exist before the nineteenth century. However, in the last lecture, Foucault does make the "deplorably banal remark about civil society" that the notion that was formerly identified with "the nation" and primarily characterized by its judicial structure "completely changed during the eighteenth century!"[32] In supporting such a "hasty remark," Foucault's own analysis is unfortunately limited to a discussion of Adam Fergusson's *Essai sur l'histoire de la société civile,* described as the "most statutory text regarding the characterization of civil society translated into French in 1783," and concerning its four essential characteristics:

> First, civil society is understood as a *historical-naturel* constant; secondly, civil society as principle of spontaneous synthesis [i.e., of a social bond that is de facto always already composed by power relations, or differences in ability and productive capacity that become their natural cause]; third, civil society as a permanent matrix of political power; fourth, civil society as the motor element history.[33]

I won't go into Foucault's summary of these four characteristics, except to point out that it reveals nothing about the concept of civil society that emerges much later at the beginning of the nineteenth century. For example, it is in the fourth essential characteristic of "the motor element of History" that we find the contributions of Hegel and Marx, where the concept of civil society will emerge directly in relation to a communitarian and spiritual existence of "the nation." (In one offhanded reference only, Foucault says, "And, of course, there is Hegel—about whom I will not speak— and the self-consciousness and ethical realization of civil society."[34]) The balance of the lecture only attempts to point out a divergence concerning the definitions of civil society and the role of governmentality—no longer identified solely with the rule of law or the personality of sovereignty but rather along highly nationalist lines between England, France, and Germany. Thus it is only in the German tradition where civil society is analyzed in direct opposition to the state-form that we might find the basis for Foucault's interest in the example of the ordoliberalism and for Rüstow's concept of *Vitalpolitik,* in particular.

Returning now to Rüstow, what he describes as the history of Western political forms is actually what he calls the evolution of a ten-thousand-year process of superstratification of societies that had reached its pinnacle in the Middle Ages in Western societies and, ever since, has been gradually degenerating between two extreme states of freedom and domination. According to this evolutionary narrative of the state-form, since this period (roughly the period of baroque Absolutism), the evolution of the modern state has primarily functioned to develop new techniques to neutralize the sharpened tensions created by the ongoing process of superstratification, mostly by legitimating the effects of domination as part of either a natural or divine order. For example, classical liberalism and the laissez-faire doctrine actually took root according to a Christian and pietistic understanding of the economy as part of God's natural design, which therefore should not be interfered with by any human agency. The invisible hand of Adam Smith was mysterious because it was the hand of God, which actually guaranteed individual liberty. This belief can also be found in Hayek's version of the market as a transcendent and posthuman entity, a collective processor of information and knowledge that surpasses any possible degree of individual knowledge and expertise. However, one result of this "theological perversion" of the economy, according to Rüstow's account of classical liberalism after the seventeenth century, is that this theological-political ideology has only proceeded "half consciously through a series of palliatives and attenuations, by way of checks and balances in the structure of domination itself."[35]

If this comes off sounding a lot like Marx's critique of classical liberalism, this is because Rüstow vindicates Marx's primary materialist thesis of the modern subject's alienation, which historically reaches its tipping point beginning in the eighteenth century and necessarily becomes "collectivized" (i.e., the "proletarianization of man"). As Rüstow writes:

> we can very largely subscribe to the socialist critique of this capitalist economy and even to Marx's thesis that this "capitalist" economy, carried further, must perforce lead to communism and collectivism. Indeed, one might even speak of "late capitalism" as an unconscious and inconsistent form of *proto-collectivism*.[36]

The only point on which Rüstow strongly disagrees with Marx's outline of "the end of Capitalism" in the *Grundrisse* (which provides the basic

teleology of many post-Marxist theories today) is that this contradic-
tion should strategically be pushed beyond the productive limit of capital itself—that is, the historical (or even eschatological) limit of capitalist
(or free market) society. As history has shown many times, however, this
strategy has encountered a final limit in the subject of individual interest,
homo economicus, which, according to Foucault's thesis, functions as *the
soul* in the highly individuated forms of human capital. Therefore, given the
sharpened consciousness around the experience of freedom (or liberty),
any coercion of interest by an external force would immediately be felt by
the subject as a form of domination, especially since, according to Rüstow,
the modern individual has been sensitized to a "pathological degree" to
any overt manifestation of power as sovereignty. Therefore, if it is to remain
effective in steering the individual form of interest to a desired collective
end, the art of government must develop new techniques of power that do
not immediately appear in the earlier forms of domination—for example,
inhibition, repression, coercion, or subjugation.

THE SOCIETY OF CONTROL

The last observation requires me to make a brief digression around Deleuze's concept of "control," which purportedly represents a new mode of
subjectification corresponding to the emergence of a new *homo economicus.*
In his 1990 "Postscript on a Society of Control," Deleuze defines the new
form of biopower as continuous and nonsegmentary (i.e., "molting," "like
a snake shedding its coils")—in other words, as "soft" or "fluid"—thus departing from a disciplinary subjectivity that was molded by "cuts" (*couperes*)
or analogical breaks (e.g., "you are no longer at home," says the teacher;
"you are no longer in school," says the corporate boss).[37] As we saw in the
previous section, the main concern of *Vitalpolitik* in shaping the values of
human capital in its highly individuated form (which Foucault describes
as "a microcosm of multiple enterprises") was to normalize the techniques
of subjectification so that the subject is gradually blended into the grain of
a free market economy without any sign of overt coercion or the potentially disintegrating pathological reaction caused by power's manifestation
as repression and violence. As we have witnessed more recently, this would
include the expansion of juridical mechanisms that seek to protect the sub-

ject of human capital from being exposed to the traumatic effects of any experience of subjection, especially in the disciplinary locations of the family,
the school, and the workplace (e.g., corporal violence, humiliation, bully-
ing, hazing, racism, sexual harassment). However, it is around this new development that we might note Deleuze's greatest concern is the fate of the
value of resistance when power loses its oppressive or violent character, no
longer appearing in the earlier guise of sovereign oppression but accessible
to a new set of rules and to new subjective technologies in the hands of
the oppressed themselves. At this point, the mechanisms of control appear
strangely liberating and might even be mistaken for a degree, or multiple
degrees, of individual and collective liberty (e.g., subjection as liberation,
incarceration as open, constant training as opportunity).[38] Consequently,
in this regard, it is important to note that the French language still allows
for a strong association between the technological meaning of "control"
(*controller*) and the sovereign figure of the master—that is, to be in control
of something or someone (*être maître*)—which, particularly in the school
and university, is an archaic figure of sovereignty that must be kept under
constant surveillance (even remote control) by the biopolitical dispositif.

In 1990, Deleuze explicitly proposes a critical program to identify
these new mechanisms of control, which he defines in terms of a new social problem: how to locate and identify all the elements of a multiplicity in
an open or relatively open, unlimited, or "smooth space." This is contrasted
to the social problem of a disciplinary diagram: how to locate a relative
number of elements of a finite multiplicity within an enclosed space or set
(e.g., the factory, the school, the prison, the hospital). If this dualism of
open versus closed spatial composition resembles the same dynamic employed earlier on in the cinema books (i.e., between the closed set first proposed by the movement-image vs. the open set linked by a line to the "outside" by the time-image), this is because he was working on both projects
around the same time as the 1985–86 lectures on Foucault.[39] Expanding
on the distinction drawn between "time-image" and "movement-image,"
for example, in the seminar, Deleuze will first theorize the difference between the two diagrams of power as precisely the problem of localization
in spatiotemporal forms in a theory of ensembles that is also referenced
with Guattari in *A Thousand Plateaus* (1980).[40] In other words, the difference between discipline and control is reduced to the spatiotemporal

distinction of enclosure (striated) versus open (smooth) spatiotemporal processes.

According to Deleuze, the specific problem of localization in the disciplinary diagram was that of a finite multiplicity and the relative localization of elements in coordinated segments or enclosures—that is, populations of masses, classes, and races are homogenous elements of a finite multiplicity localized according to a diagram of enclosure (e.g., villages or ghettoes in the city, zones or shantytowns in a district, regions or even continents in the diagram of globalization). Each finite multiplicity operates according to the analogy provided by the disciplinary diagram to localize the elements or population that belonged to that set. However, according to Deleuze, the problem of localization "coming into view" (circa 1980s) under the name of control is no longer a finite multiplicity that is localized in enclosures but rather what in the seminar on Foucault he defines as an "*unlimited finity* [*sic*]" dispersed across an open and nonstriated space (i.e., no longer individuals but privatized markets, databanks, localized enterprises). In other words, what is being presented as a diagram of control mechanism is nothing other than "Riemannian patches of space devoid of any kind of homogeneity."⁴¹ As Deleuze and Guattari write, "each [space] is characterized by the form of the expression that defines the square of the distance between two infinitely proximate points so that two neighboring observers in a Riemann space can locate the points in their immediate vicinity but cannot locate their spaces in relation to each other without a new convention [i.e., a new dispositif]."⁴²

If we now observe the same phenomenon as described in the "Postscript," written just ten years later, it is precisely the emergence of a new dispositif based on the same principle of openness that will suddenly become the source of Deleuze's greatest fears. This is because he will also notice the invention of newer technical machines (the internet, databanks, electronic collars) that emerge to recode these unformed elements outside disciplinary enclosures and establish localization once again, even though this localization no longer occurs through an apparatus or territorial enclosure. To illustrate this apparent danger, we could simply point to the famous example that Deleuze ascribes to Guattari the prisoner, who is no longer enclosed in a disciplinary space but rather allowed to remain in open society under the condition that his location is electronically monitored. Stripped of its practical application as a cheaper and more cost-efficient form of confinement (especially for nonviolent offenders, petty criminals, and juvenile delinquents), all that would be required is simply the addition of what Deleuze and Guattari refer to as a "qualitative leap" whereby this technology would become applied universally, as in the case, for example, of Guattari's description of a city with districts controlled by digital pass codes or biometric tags, thus becoming a "machinic form of enslavement."[43]

It is not at all surprising that Deleuze's description of a "society of control" now acquires the distinctive feeling (a mood, or *melos*) of science fiction, since it is precisely by means of a model that is borrowed from this genre that Foucault's previous description of the nineteenth-century disciplinary order undergoes a strange mutation into the emergent dispositif of control, specifically by providing it with a supplemental and strategic dimension of a diabolical power that is "coming from the future" (i.e., "the confinement of the outside"). Moreover, the reference to science fiction is not purely accidental either. In a footnote that appears in *A Thousand Plateaus,* we find the following statement: "One of the basic themes of science fiction is to show how machinic enslavement combines with processes of subjection, but exceeds or differs from them, performing *a qualitative leap.*"[44] This qualitative leap is more clearly stated by Neil Gaiman in his introduction to Bradbury's *Fahrenheit 451* as the principle of the "what-if" hypothesis in the science fiction method for the creation of possible worlds. Gaiman summarizes this method as follows:

There are three phrases that make possible the world of writing about the world of not-yet (you can call it science fiction or speculative fiction; you can call it anything you wish) and they are simple phrases: What if . . . ? If only . . . If this goes on . . . "What if . . . ?" gives us change, a departure from our lives. (What if aliens landed tomorrow and gave us everything we wanted, but at a price?) "If only . . ." lets us explore the glories and dangers of tomorrow. (If only dogs could talk. If only I were invisible.) "If this goes on . . ." is the most predictive of the three, although it doesn't try to predict an actual future with all its messy confusion. Instead, "If this goes on . . ." fiction takes an element of life today, something clear and obvious and normally something troubling, and asks what would happen if that thing, that one thing, became bigger, became all-pervasive, changed the way we thought and behaved. (If this goes on, all communication everywhere will be through text messages or computers, and direct speech between two people, without a machine, will be outlawed.)[45]

Here we can clearly see the same method Deleuze uses to create his image of control. Thus applying the third method of "If this goes on . . ." to Foucault's earlier descriptions of the mechanisms of discipline, and then linking these disciplines to the newer technical machines (e.g., text messages, Twitter), one can easily create a possible world simply by totalizing the relationship between a technical form of subjection and what Deleuze and Guattari call "a machinic form of enslavement." According to this same method, "social subjection now proportions itself to the model of realization, just as machinic enslavement expands to meet the dimensions of an axiomatic that is effectuated in the model."[46]

It is by the same method that in the opening of the "Postscript," Deleuze basically updates a postwar dystopian vision of control that is drawn from a short story by Ray Bradbury with a more psychedelic version of the new form of subjection that is drawn from William Burroughs's sublimely paranoid vision. Accordingly, control is far more insidious in that it is constituted at the level of neuronal and chemical signals in the brain itself; the so-called *dividual* would not be able to discern the difference between messages that are organically spontaneous and messages (or thoughts and desires) that are actually communicated by a new race of "Senders." According to Deleuze's use of this analogy to define the problem of thinking in a "society of control," the "Senders" are simply represented by an impudent breed of new masters: the media and advertising men. Social subjection now proportions itself to the dispositif of control, because all the subjects have internalized the space of confinement that belonged to the former disciplinary apparatus, which has now become a new "machinic form of enslavement." For example, Maurice Blanchot also defined this new form of subjection as a form of confinement that refers to an indeterminate exteriority and not to the nucleus of interiority or enclosure; hence confinement refers to an outside, and what is confined is the outside itself.[47]

The real question now becomes, as Deleuze observes, how to reunite the two very different diagrams of the dispositif, especially when the dispositifs themselves are always already in a process of mutation. In the seminar of 1986, Deleuze observes:

> First, I would say, the diagram arrives from the outside, although we do not know exactly what Foucault understands by "the outside." Secondly, the diagram always emerges from another diagram. And why? Because every diagram is a mutation! Every diagram is the mutation of

the preceding one, which was itself already a mutation. The diagram is fundamentally mutant and even expresses, within a given society, the mutations that are possible. Thus, the question is one of reuniting the two [dispositifs].[48]

On the other hand, Foucault's description of the relationship between the disciplinary apparatus and the dispositif of control cannot be understood in terms of the difference between an ideal and a real model. As Dean and Villadsen have recently argued, the history of the dispositifs is not one that demonstrates their remarkable endurance and success in capturing all social space but rather a history that can also be defined as "plans never realized." Consequently, "Foucault gives emphasis to the fundamentally unattainable nature of diagrams and their imperatives, comparing them to 'a programming left in abeyance.'"[49] Contrary to this understanding of the nature of power and its inability to realize itself in concrete dispositifs, Deleuze's description of the new forms of subjection completely realizes the model of discipline and manages to totalize the social field outside the former spaces of confinement (e.g., the prison replaced by GPS tracking device, the proletariat ghetto by digitalized access on a *dividual* level, the school by constant training in personal electives, the freedom to think by Twitter).[50] The ideal model of control is thus portrayed as the realization of a machinic form of enslavement that expands to include all social space, somewhat like an alien invasion in science fiction films, because it now operates in a completely different dimension than the earlier concrete or technical dispositifs. Here, I believe, we have discovered the primary distinction that defines the axiomatic of control society: the form of subjection no longer needs a specific apparatus but instead has incorporated or confined a dimension of *the outside*, "which is farther away than any external world and even any form of exteriority" and, for this reason, is "infinitely closer and deeper than any form of interiority as well."[51] Consequently, as in the case of Agamben's description of the technological dispositif (i.e., cell phones, internet, etc.), there is no escape or resistance, because the outside is already found to be on the inside.

Of course, I am intentionally exaggerating the theory of control, but clearly this demonstrates the problem of the earlier models and diagrams that are like old programs of sovereignty left in abeyance and that function a bit like old portraits of power (I will return to describing them in the conclusion). I also realize that I risk turning Deleuze into a "straw man," or at least into what he already confesses himself to be at the end of his "Post-Scriptum," "an old mole, a little blind to the intricacies of the snake's coil." [52] Although I said that this would be a digression, the epistemological question that should concern us is that the dualism between "two spatiotemporal diagrams of power" can nowhere be found in Foucault's own descriptions of disciplinary order, nor in his descriptions of the nature of power that is emerging within the biopolitical dispositif. Moreover, I would simply judge Deleuze's later reaction to the influence of neoliberal policies in France through the 1980s under the banner of "Control Society" and suggest that a better term for understanding the new principle of governmentality that is emerging after disciplinary society might be an "Enterprise" rather than "Control." What then is the relationship between what Foucault calls "Enterprise Society" (or "Control Society") and a Judicial Society (or, perhaps, a Disciplinary Society)? Recalling the above passage where Foucault observes the "multiple surfaces of friction" that emerge within neoliberal society, these are also identified as the intersection of new techniques and new forms of subjectivity. However, these subjectivities do not necessarily immediately lead to new forms of potential resistance, or "counterattack," according to the formalist analogy with serialization in music or to the syntactic and linguistic discoveries of writers like Raymond Roussel, whom Deleuze employs as a kind of cryptic key to decipher Foucault's writings on power after *Discipline and Punish*.[53] Instead, what we are witnessing is nothing less than a mutation of Foucault's earlier conception of biopower that belonged to the dispositif of sexuality but which is exaggerated to take "life itself" as its direct object.[54] ("Life becomes resistance to power when power takes life as its object.")[55] To my knowledge, however, Foucault nowhere makes such a global statement concerning the direct object of the biopolitical dispositif—at least, not without rehearsing a number of epistemological qualifications concerning what he defines as the "concrete assemblages" of new techniques and knowledges that will compose the "government of the living."

THE PROBLEM OF AN "INFLATIONARY THEORY OF THE STATE"

After a brief digression into the genre of science fiction, I will now conclude in returning to Foucault's more sober and realistic view concerning one possible future of power relations, or at least, its immediate past. My first observation is that the theoretical problem that the 1978–79 lectures actually seek to address is neither the spatiotemporal arrangement of the diagram of control nor the future of power itself (because power is not an essence) but rather a specifically historical or genealogical problem: the causal factors behind a significant divergence of the classical liberal doctrine in the postwar years, primarily between a European-style liberalism, in which the rule of law limits state sovereignty over economic relations, and an American-style liberalism, in which an ideal theory of the state is to protect individual liberties and the collective pursuit of happiness. In both cases, Foucault also finds a specific and populist phenomenon of what he calls "state phobia": in Europe, it is the ongoing fear of centralization of the economy within the state apparatus (e.g., socialism, communism); in America, it is the suspicion concerning the collusion between the state apparatus and private enterprise (e.g., monopolies, corporatism, the "military–industrial complex").

My second observation is that this philosophical division is only further complicated in the postwar period when European emigrants like Hayek, on the extreme right, and members of the Frankfurt School, on the far left, effectively import a European style of "state phobia" into the American universities and privately funded "policy centers" (in the case of Hayek and the Volker Fund at the University of Chicago). This will lead to what Foucault refers to as "an inflationary theory of the state-form" on both continents, one that has different imaginary coordinates but that will become a constant feature of the politics on both continents in the postwar period. I will argue that this "inflationary theory" continues to influence the contemporary framework of political theory, especially concerning the relationship between the state-form and neoliberal society in recent leftist theory in North America, and thus it is a primary factor in explaining the negative reception of Foucault's earlier lectures on the principles of neoliberal governmentality.[56]

Recalling our discussion concerning the notions of the strong versus the weak state-form vis-à-vis Rüstow and Hayek, Foucault also underlines this aspect in his discussion of what he calls the "state phobia" as the basis for interpreting the psychology of émigrés like Hayek, but also of leftist political émigrés affiliated with the Frankfurt School (Horkheimer, Adorno, Arendt, Marcuse, Lowenthal, etc.). He writes:

This phobia had many agents and promoters, from economics profes-
sors inspired by Austrian neo-marginalism [here Foucault is explicitly
referring to Ludwig von Mises, who emigrated to the United States in
1940 through a grant by the Rockefeller Foundation and was later supported by the Volker Fund], to political exiles who, from 1920–1925,
have certainly played a major role in the formation of contemporary political consciousness, a role that perhaps has not been studied closely
enough. An entire political history of exile could be written, or a history
of exile and its ideological, theoretical, and practical effects.[57]

At this point, following our discussion in the last section, we might also include in this "political history of exile" the writings of Deleuze and Guattari
themselves. Of course, the fact that they were not political exiles does not
mean they that do not always write from a position of the "outsider," as in
the case of the schizophrenic and the nomad. In fact, this recalls Jameson's
early critique of Deleuze and Guattari in *The Political Unconscious* (1981)
as ideological dupes for the emerging neoliberal order of late-capitalist
commodity culture, if not unwittingly its "double agents" in the unconscious of the American left following the 1970s, who, by the early 1980s,
had migrated into American universities and were reading the collected
works of the members of the Frankfurt School alongside a well-worn copy
of *Anti-Oedipus*.[58]

What Jameson is criticizing is the same phenomenon of "state phobia" that Foucault observed in roughly the same moment, which he also
ascribed to the influence of "foreign agents" in the United States who mud-
died the different national contexts in the history of liberalism in Europe
and the United States. For Jameson, this produces in the cultural unconscious of the American left, especially in the Reagan era, "the real problem
about the importation and translation of theoretical polemics which have
a quite different semantic content than the national situation in which they
originate."[59] For example, his argument is that the polarity between a centralized form of politics and "molecular" forms of individual and collective
interests located in civil society is reversed in the process of translation from
the one national context to the other, that is, from the European context
to the U.S. context. What Rüstow had earlier called "proto-collectivism,"
specifically in reaction to the centralization of politics in the state-form in
European societies, is identified by Jameson in 1981 as the major obstacle

to any alliance politics forming among the different splinter groups of the American left (e.g., "ethnic groups, neighborhood movements, feminism, various 'counter-cultural' or alternative life-style groups, rank and file labor dissidence, student movements, single-issue movements"), which, together, "project demands and strategies that are theoretically incompatible and impossible to coordinate on any practical political basis."[60] Of course, this splintering has only continued to expand and intensify; moreover, as I have suggested in the opening of this study, the function of the polemics within theoretical discourse isolated in the university, for the most part, has only further emaciated and weakened the meaning of the "political" today. In my view, recalling Jameson's earlier critique, this only proves that we still have some unfinished business to settle with our "political unconscious."

Returning to our subject, and to the particular historical moment that Foucault and Jameson were both addressing from opposite shores of the pond, the real problem is how to explain the convergence of the same, if not the identical, principle of "state phobia" among both conservative proponents of neoliberal doctrine on the right and the "antisystemic" critics of totalization on the left, but without simply reducing it, as Jameson does, to a symptomatic and unconscious importation of European ideology. Of course, it might appear more than a little counterintuitive that Deleuze and Guattari would see as the greatest threat the very same thing that most neoliberal economic theorists in the same period also viewed with fear and loathing: the return of a "strong" or centralized state-form, such as the prewar welfare state of Roosevelt or Keynes. In addition, there are different historical state-forms, some of which are deemed to be good or bad a priori (fascist, nationalist, socialist-democratic, communist, totalitarian), but there is also a kind of universal assumption that the state itself is the only political mechanism that is imaginable in the exercise of political power. (This can be illustrated in recent nostalgia for the return of some version of the "national welfare state" as the only solution available on the contemporary horizon of neoliberal society today.[61]) One usually begins by assuming the existence of the state, and then of a particular state-form judged to be either beneficial or threatening—even if, as in the most extreme example of Deleuze and Guattari, this assumes the form of an *Urstaat* that is always lurking beneath every political mechanism as its insidious underside, or "apparatus of capture." As they say, "we always come back to the idea of the

State that comes into the world fully formed and rises up in a single stroke, the unconditioned *Urstaat.*"[62] In a certain sense, viewed from the historical perspective of American liberalism, this expression of state phobia is not that different from the classical conspiracy between the state and the "military–industrial complex" (i.e., the "war machine").

It is around the nature of this "axiomatic presupposition" that a critical observation should be made with regard to Foucault's own attempt in the same period "to do without a theory of the state," that is, to not be forced to choose a particular state-form to begin his analysis of the techniques of governmentality. As he explains in the lecture of January 31, 1979, this means "not starting off with an analysis of the nature, structure, and function of the state in and for itself, if it means not starting off from the state considered as a political universal," and then deducing the status of political and moral questions from this presupposition of the state-form, for good or ill.[63] In other words, it is the privileged state-form that one assumes at the very beginning of the analysis of power, or in the critique of political economy, that will ultimately determine which state-form one ends up rationalizing, regardless of whether such a state actually exists, or whether it even existed in the past, or the horrible human costs associated with its previous historical incarnations. This merely recapitulates his earlier manner of investigating the question of political power as such by first avoiding (or "bypassing") the axiom of sovereignty in constructing an analytic of power relations. Instead, Foucault describes the state-form as nothing more than the profile of a mobile figure in perpetual movement, which can perhaps be best illustrated by Kafka's description of *The Castle*, which, from the perspective of a very great distance, appears as a gigantic Behemoth, but, as you draw closer, in reality is only a thousand ramshackle huts stuck on a hillside. Thus, according to this perspectivism, "the state is nothing else but the mobile effect of the regime of multiple governmentalities."[64]

It follows from this "axiomatized" analysis of multiple governmentalities, which does not assume the presence of a centralized state-form, that in the lectures of this period, he clearly rejects many of the contemporary leftist and Marxist interpretations of neoliberalism on the basis that these critiques already start out with a "theory of the state" and then reduce or exaggerate the state's actual role in any number of claims (e.g., "Adam Smith,

Marx, Solzhenitsyn, *laissez-faire* capitalism, society of the spectacle, the *'mondialisation'* of the concentration camp, the Gulag, the *Urstaat,* etc.").[65] This is what he calls the problem of "an inflationary theory of the state," or, simply put, "state phobia." According to this style of criticism, as Foucault rightly observes concerning his own contemporary moment, the state becomes responsible for everything and, thus, is empirically responsible for almost "nothing at all, repeating the same kind of critique for the last two hundred, one hundred years, or even the last ten years."[66] Broadly speaking, therefore, these are the analytical and critical frameworks in which the emerging principles of neoliberalism were being interpreted by his own contemporaries at the end of the 1970s, including Deleuze and Guattari, as we have seen. And for the most part, *it is within the same analytical framework that the entire phenomenon is still being interpreted today, nearly forty years later*!

So, ultimately, what is wrong with "an inflationary theory of the state-form"? Foucault's comments seem to imply—at least as an analytical framework—that it has no epistemological value for either real historical analysis or effective political critique of actual state-forms or the techniques of governmentality. In the following, therefore, I will attempt to boil down Foucault's four main criticisms for comparison with the contemporary analytical framework:

(a) The first criticism concerns what I have already revealed as the fundamental presupposition in Deleuze and Guattari's own analysis of the history of the state-form, that is, the "axiom" that the state has existed from the very beginning only to function as "a model of realization." What does the state-form realize according to this model? The answer, following Marx and Engels, is the "capitalist axiomatic." Of course, as we are told, the axiomatic is much more complex today than it was in the nineteenth century, but basically the principle of axiomatization refers to the manner in which the state-form as a model, even from its very beginning in the feudal state, has always "secretly" operated to realize the axiomatic in the "last instance" (Althusser). Moreover, with the emergence of neoliberalism, we now witness a framework that expands to include all of society, which is why in the previous section I described the difference between a technical machine of subjection and a "machinic form of enslavement." However, this new framework is no longer composed of the state, or actual political mechanisms, but, following Louis Mumford, a "meta-stable economic framework composed of interchangeable parts, organic and inorganic, human and animal, technical and institutional, that are organized and controlled by universal markets" (i.e., a "mega-machine").[67]

(b) The second criticism concerns what Foucault calls the problem of the interchangeability of analyses according to a hereditary model of kinship.[68] One result of employing a genetic or hereditary model of kinship—*as is the case when any biological model is applied to analogically real historical phenomena!*—is that the understanding of specific causality is often reduced to a reproduction of paradigms and archetypal forms. In other words, anytime you begin with a genetic kinship between different forms of the state, for example, from the standpoint of a Universal History of Capitalism, these become eternal forms that can be reactivated at any point of the great chain of being, thus sacrificing any possible specificity in the analysis of the circumstances of the specific genesis or coming into being of actual states by proposing instead a hereditary model of evolution. Once again, to take what Foucault at this point calls a "critical commonplace frequently found today," this hereditary model is clearly present in Deleuze and Guattari's division of the history of the state-form into three species that can be reactualized in various hybrid combinations from the perspective of Universal History. But the hereditary model is especially figured in their assertion that the most primitive state-form, the archaic imperial or "Oriental despotic form," which is derived from early Marx, constitutes the absolute horizon of each historical transformation.[69] In other words, there is the presence of an organic model of heredity and evolution, which is more than a little responsible for the organicism implicit in the concept of biopower that has been derived mostly from Deleuze's writings. Moreover, their analysis cannot account for the differences that occur within each generic species, which cannot be grouped under the same hereditary scheme, and this is particularly true in the case of the second major genre under the subspecies of "extremely diverse states" (monarchies, feudal systems, evolved empires, autonomous cities, etc.), and the resulting loss of specificity or the dilution of differences between actual state-forms of the same genre or species can certainly be applied to the third species (i.e., the modern nation-states). For example, in addition to Deleuze and Guattari, here we might also recall the argument of Hardt and Negri, who employ the same scheme of Universal History of the state-form, which they take directly from Deleuze and Guattari, to describe the reactualization of the "autonomous *polis*" in their description of the new form of Empire created by the Multitude.[70]

(c) The third criticism could be summarized according to the principle of the "worst of the worst," according to either the biopolitical model of machinic enslavement or the nuclear threat of the total extinction of humanity, which is the secret fantasy of the state itself. This directly results from the interchangeability of analyses and makes possible the reactualization of the most extreme and despotic state-form in place of any actual state-form with its police forms of power. For example, "certain European police forces could be taken as an example, when they claim the right to 'shoot on sight': they cease to be a cogwheel in the State apparatus and become pieces in a war machine."[71] Therefore every finite instance of state power (such as police violence) is immediately referred to as the "return of fascism." Foucault addresses this inflationary tendency in current political theory most directly: "For example, an analysis of social security and the administrative apparatus on which it rests ends up, via some slippages and thanks to some play on words, referring to the analysis of concentration camps."[72] Recalling the second characteristic of hereditary kinship, moreover, because the intrinsic dynamism of the state-form has internalized its entire hereditary past in each instance of state power and violence, the every actual instance of legal violence or the juridical expression of state power immediately evokes the realization of the axiom of the "worst of the worst." As Foucault writes, "it hardly matters what one's grasp of the reality is or what profile of actuality is really present. Mere suspicion is enough evidence for denunciation, to find something like the fantastical profile of the state and there is no longer any need to analyze."[73] As the most extreme example of this inflationary model, we should recall that Foucault begins his analysis of state phobia by directly linking the fear of the state to the invention of the atomic bomb. As he writes, in the immediate postwar period, "one of the most constant features is the coupling of this fear [of the state] with the fear of the atomic bomb. The state and the atomic bomb, or the bomb rather than the state, or the state is no better than the bomb, or the state entails the bomb, or the bomb necessarily entails and calls for the state."[74]

(d) Finally, the fourth criticism concerns what I have already described as the mythic return of the *Urstaat,* that is to say, according to the model of what I would call the *great paranoid state-form* (in reference to Suetonius's account of the twelve great paranoids of the Roman Empire). However, in reality, this inflationary theory is only the outcome of the first two critical commonplaces, since one no longer even needs to concern oneself with the empirical analysis of any particular mechanism of state power, because the state-form is immediately denounced for being intrinsically and essentially despotic, fascist, totalitarian, and so on. I believe that Foucault's criticism is relevant because the appeal to an intrinsic and immanent paradigm of despotism in each case only serves to mythologize the actual mechanisms of power, especially because there is no attempt to base this kind of analysis on the actual legal codes or jurisprudence, to see how this violence is made possible and really comes about in a given situation; rather, it resorts to a kind of inductive reasoning where the event serves only as an example of the most archaic and primitive of models as what it immediately demonstrates—that is, that with every incident of police violence, the state is "becoming fascist," that its new technical machines are in the process of becoming machinic forms of enslavement, that the ultimate destination of global markets is to place all life in a concentration camp on a global scale, that the war machine will find its complete object in the menacing peace that is "worse than fascist death," and so on.[75]

To summarize all of these inflationary tendencies in the critical theory of the last forty years, I will again refer to a passage from Kafka: "The Castle hill was hidden, veiled in mist and darkness, nor was there even a glimmer of light to show that a castle was there. . . . K. stood for a long time gazing into the illusory emptiness above him."[76] In other words, it is only from the perspective of an unfathomable distance, or from a night of impenetrable fog, that the state-form itself becomes a kind of illusory presence that appears behind everything, even though one can only imagine the shadowy profile of this presence.

How does this problem of perspectivism apply to the profile of the neoliberal form of government, which is often the profile of a presence that appears behind every actual state-form, whether in the figure of an *Urstaat* or merely as the most generalized fear of capitalism? In response, let us return to the lecture of January 31, 1979, where Foucault specifically defines the problem of neoliberalism as how the overall exercise of political power can be modeled on the principles of the market economy but, at the same time, is "not the question of creating an empty space."[77] What does he mean here by the creation of an "empty space" (i.e., in the manner of Adam Smith and classical liberalism) except a certain perspective of surveillance and control that is external to the classical mechanisms of state power? Here Foucault announces that what he actually intended to investigate was the "ideal theory" of classical liberalism, meaning an ideal that has never been actualized but is more like a "program in abeyance" and is bound up with the historical problem in the evolution of the state: "the effect, the profile, the mobile shape of statification or statifications, in the sense of the incessant transactions which modify, or move, or drastically change, or insidiously shift the sources of finance, modes of investment, decision-making centers, forms and types of control, relationships between local powers, the central authority, and so on."[78]

At this point, Foucault also refers to the model of disciplinary apparatus invented by Bentham, which is also the main paradigm of *Discipline and Punish*: panopticism. However, when he invokes this model again in the 1979 lecture, four years later, it is not to say that it has been surpassed by something new but rather that the technique of the panopticon actually represents the ideal model of the state-form according to a classical theory of liberalism, a state-form that is reduced to the role of administrative surveillance, and its powers of intervention into civil society are thus restricted by its distance from market relations themselves. As Foucault writes concerning the end of Bentham's life, "panopticism is not a regional mechanics limited to certain institutions [i.e., it is not limited to prisons or to the penal system only]; for Bentham, panopticism really is a general political formula that characterizes a type of governmentality."[79] In other words, here we find that there is no break between the dispositifs of discipline and control but rather only the gradual evolution of new techniques and technologies according to an "ideal" theory of a society based on market relations, including the advances of the science of economics itself as a new technique of governing without invoking the sovereign function of state power. In other words, neoliberal policy does not project itself into an "empty space" outside the state to then fashion the mechanisms of

market society from an objective distance of an Archimedean point, because this would imply a form of economic planning and a classical state-
form of control. According to Mirowski, this explains why the neoliberal
movement must seek to consolidate political power by operating from
within the state and not as a new political ideology that appears opposed to
it.[80] But this also explains why neoliberalism has never fashioned a coherent ideology: its principles have been adapted and conformed to the different national centers by economic policy experts, thus it is famously incon-
sistent and even contradictory at times. The critical problem that concerns
us is whether, and at what point, an ideal theory of discipline becomes a
concrete strategy of control.

In conclusion, recalling again the statement by Hayek quoted earlier
on that "the individual cannot activate its species being [its biopolitical
value] by participating in the polis," it is only through participation in the
economy that the real value of any living being is determined—not only
in the form of human capital but in the biopolitical value of other species
beings as well. Nevertheless, it is also around this apparent weakening of
some—*though, certainly not all!*—of the state's sovereign power that the
contemporary neoliberal form of government has shown its powers to
defend or to protect not only to be severely weakened but no longer to
be premised on a universal form of Right, nor even a form of Right according to members of the same species being (e.g., humanism). In short,
what we are witnessing today is the multiplication of new subjects who
may have economic rights, and maybe even juridical rights, but no political rights, or whose political rights are not activated by the degree of participation in the *polis* but only to the degree of their participation in the
global market.

Foucault's own prognosis of the contemporary neoliberal society is
neither completely paranoid nor entirely distopian, moreover, but rather
concerns the change in the traditional liberal notions of individual liberty
according to a new mode of governmentality that was coming into view
at the end of the 1970s (not only in the United States but in France and
the rest of the world as well). Thus Foucault only examines three national
models of neoliberal governmentality, all of which have very different
points of emphasis and ideologies, but which all share the same "grid of
economic intelligibility." But this model has taken several detours caused
by events that occurred after this moment, perhaps even in a manner that

might cause Foucault's own analysis to be regarded as patently outdated and thus incapable of addressing the current neoliberal forms of govern-mentality, which have become nonnationally specific in the growth and dissemination of current global markets. Moreover, to say that neoliberal-ism is a problem of market policy applied within the existing framework of state mechanisms, and not an "empty space," is not completely true con-cerning the dispersion of the American style of new-liberal policy from the 1980s onward. (For example, Foucault does not mention—in fact, he may not have been aware of—the direct involvement of members of the Chicago School with the Pinochet government in Chile, including Hayek's participation in writing a new constitution, much of which is drawn from the arguments that appear in his paper "The Principles of a Liberal Social Order.") In fact, the Chicago School found such an empty space in Chile at the end of the 1970s, just as the German ordoliberals had earlier found an "empty space" in the ruins of postwar Germany twenty years before, and as members of the Mont Pèlerin Society continued to find in the decolo-nized regions of Africa, Korea, Indonesia, and Latin America throughout the 1980s and 1990s.

Given our twenty-twenty hindsight of the "art of neoliberal govern-mentality" today, I would simply point out that there is something, or a number of things, that Foucault himself could not see in 1979, much of which would seriously contradict many of his own observations—basically, that is, everything that has occurred after 1984, including the return of a laissez-faire form of capitalism on a global scale, and even the return of earlier and even archaic state-forms, including the return of the sovereign state-form in the case of then recent "strong man" figures such as Vladimir Putin, Xi Jinping, Kim Jong-un, and, last, Donald Trump. Thus we might conclude by recalling Foucault's own foreboding of the return of an archaic form of sovereignty founded on blood and sexuality (i.e., racism) in the conclusion of the first volume of *The History of Sexuality,* alongside De-leuze and Guattari's 1984 premonition of the rise of a state war machine like a creature from science fiction, which will prosecute globally "a total war against an unknown and unspecified enemy."[81] It would only take two decades for both their fears to become realized, *but this is a contemporary reality stripped of all science fiction!* But, in the end, that is another geneal-ogy, and the future portended by this most contemporary return of our sovereign figure remains, in most accounts, through a glass darkly.

Article III
On the Mutations of Biopower
(Post-1984)

As Descartes defined it, in a synthetic method of presentation, one works backward from the conclusion, usually beginning from "common notions" and then running through each step of the analysis to arrive at an adequate knowledge of the subject (in this case, the subject of biopower). A drawback of this manner of presentation is that it risks restating things that are already known beforehand and even redundancy around certain points that have been sufficiently covered already. A second drawback is that for the inattentive reader who skips over any step in the demonstration, it risks giving the impression that one can simply arrive at the conclusion and walk away from the whole matter having learned more than she really has. As for a third kind of drawback, for the polemical reader who is too busy looking for counterarguments, I will simply quote Descartes, who said, "I think I can fairly give the back of my hand to the worthless verdict given by those who stick to their preconceived ideas on the subject and refuse to meditate a little while with me."[1]

Therefore let me begin (again) by highlighting the importance of Foucault's two great methodological reversals in the analysis of the subject of power: first, to no longer define power through a traditional theory of sovereignty or philosophy of right. Second, as Foucault states at many points throughout his analysis of the subject of power, we must not imagine that power is either an eternal form or a natural being. Rather, it is "an artifice, a device, a technique, or a strategy." Thus, after subtracting the natural and historical representations of power—first of all, that power is not an attribute, that is, neither substance, as in Spinoza, nor subject, as in Hegel and Marx—we arrive at the following definition first given in the first volume of *The History of Sexuality* (1976): "power is not an institution, and not a structure; neither is it a certain strength we are endowed with; it is the name that one attributes to a complex strategic situation in a particular society."[2]

Beginning with the lectures of 1975–76, in his analysis of the subject of power, Foucault announces that he will no longer privilege the juridical model of contract theory, because power is not something that can first be possessed and subsequently "alienated" like property or a commodity. Therefore the description of "power as a right that can be possessed in the same way one possesses a commodity" only functions in reference to a juridical model that rationalizes the transfer and accumulation of power in certain social subjects and classes and its alienation (or "scarcity") in others; as a result, beginning in the nineteenth century, "political power finds its historical *raison d'etre* in the economy."[3] This is the principle at the basis of what Foucault later describes in the lectures on *The Birth of Biopolitics,* following Hume and British empiricism, as a new subject beginning in the eighteenth century, *homo economicus,* in distinction from *homo juridicus,* the subject of right.[4]

Turning to the first appearance of the concept of "biopower" in the lectures of 1975, Foucault introduces the emergence of "a new power of normalization,"[5] something he goes on to define variously as both a new "element" and a new "technique of which the theory of right and disciplinary practice knew nothing."[6] This is because the theory of right only treated individuals (in particular, "individual citizens") and the assumption of an implicit social contract between them, and disciplines only treated their bodies in practical terms (as living, laboring, reproducing, etc.); whereas, as Foucault states, "what we are dealing with in the new technology of power is not exactly society . . . nor the individual-as-body" but rather an entirely new and multiple body of the population as both a statistical and biological problem of power from that point onward.[7]

Foucault's foregoing understanding of the character of power is primarily drawn from the biologist-philosopher Georges Canguilhem. Foucault applies Canguilhem's groundbreaking interpretation in *The Normal and the Pathological* (1966), in which the power of the norm is first defined as something that operates differently from law, because "the norm's function is not to exclude and reject but rather is always linked to a positive technique of intervention and transformation of the population."[8] This insight directly leads to Foucault's adaptation of the evolution of the norm to determine the technical apparatus of discipline as something that is patently "artificial," like a machine, but which, like any machine, demands constant reinvention, adaptation, correction, and new techniques and tactics, and which is also vulnerable to sudden interruptions, appropriations, captures, breakdowns, and even sudden reversals.

It is also at this point that a model of biological normalization is substituted for mechanical causality to determine the evolutionary path of any normative order as also being open to the moments of rupture and discontinuity, as well as the sudden appearance of new elements and techniques, as part of a generalized struggle to maintain its consistency and unity. Foucault employs this new model as a lever to pry the analysis of power away from a classical mechanistic and even modern structural determination of power; hence the subject of power no longer exclusively refers to a positive and heterogeneous agency of the law or to a sovereign figure but also functions as a normative autonomous agency.[9] It is here we find the convergence of two techniques that will later be employed to define the dual object of any biopolitical order: strategies directed toward populations and concrete techniques directed at the "granular" level of individual subjectivities.

A year later, Foucault will recount a different starting point for his genealogy of biopower in the first volume of *The History of Sexuality*, indicating both a different direction of his research and a slightly different problem, which is the abstract body of normative power that suddenly appears as the real target of the process defined earlier on by the array of disciplinary techniques and apparatuses recounted in *Discipline and Punish*, but then just as quickly disappears into the enigma of the dispositif of sexuality. In other words, following the explosion of numerous and diverse techniques for subjugating bodies, the "age of biopower" could only be said to have properly commenced when the two understandings of power that were still separated by the end of the eighteenth century, and were only joined at the level of discourse (i.e., "ideology"), gradually converged in the "concrete assemblages" *(agencements concrets)* of power beginning in the nineteenth century.

To account for this sudden convergence and transformation, we must again highlight Foucault's dual use of the terms *element* and *technique* in his presentation of the concept of biopower. For example, sexuality can be described as an element (in the sense of a medium) that is crucial to the incipient development of later capitalism (the insertion of actual bodies into the machinery of production and, at the same time, the optimization of life, habits, and health of general populations) but is also a technique that is deployed as part of an overall strategy of power. This would imply, as Foucault argues, that what is now called "sexuality" from the nineteenth century onward can no longer be understood to belong to the "body" understood as an exterior domain to which power is applied but rather as "a complex idea" that takes shape inside the different strategies of power that will determine what subjective role that sexuality will play—that is, as being both the element of a "concrete assemblage" (dispositif) and, at the same time, an abstract and hidden figure of power's overall design.[10]

In presenting the complex idea of sexuality, which is initially defined as an "artificial unity" of heterogeneous elements in more generalizable strategies of subjection and subjectification, Foucault provides the first concrete description of one of the most powerful "biopolitical dispositifs." It is also important to recall, however, that at the same moment, sexuality was being hailed as the very fulcrum of subjectivity, given its practical and theoretical function established by Freudian psychoanalysis. Thus, recalling another famous hypothesis that also appears in the opening of *The History of Sexuality,* the forms of subjectification *(formes d'assujettissement)* do not always appear in the form of repression or inhibition (based largely on an earlier theory of the instincts) but rather also through more positive forms of incitement, seduction, multiplication, and expansion. Foucault will return to this hypothesis later, in 1982, two years before his death, to announce a new problem of power that concerns precisely the explosion of new forms of subjectification. He says that even though the struggles against forms of domination and oppression have certainly not disappeared—"in fact, quite the opposite!"—it is what he defines as the "submission to subjectivity itself" (that is to say, the coercive normative forms of subjection and subjectivity, such as race and sexuality) that may be responsible for producing the greatest resistances today.[11]

Concerning the 1978–79 lectures, it is important to point out once again that while Foucault first sets out to examine the emergence of this new "political economy" of biopolitics, which has become associated with the overall techniques of a neoliberal form of governmentality, by the mid-point of the year, he restricts his analysis mostly to the German postwar policy of "social market theory." This raises the question of whether the lecture course of 1978–79 actually provides us with a complete picture of the so-called birth of biopolitics, or even a coherent theory of the *biopolitical dispositif* that governs contemporary neoliberal societies, as many of Foucault's contemporary readers have assumed. If only viewed from a historical perspective, the answer would clearly be no. In fact, Foucault's own analysis might even be viewed as historically dated, because it cannot account for significant divergences in neoliberal doctrine that did not occur until the mid-1980s, along with the rise of Thatcherism and Reagonomics in the mid-1980s; thus his analysis of American neoliberalism extends only to the end of the Carter administration and cannot address the current phenomenon of neoliberalism that has expanded globally since then. On the other hand, does this necessarily imply that Foucault's analysis provides us with no tools for understanding the nature of neoliberal governmentality today? Here the answer would also be "no." That is to say, we should assess the value of Foucault's analytic as providing us with what he called "a grid of intelligibility" for studying a new model of economic rationality. In other words, as I have demonstrated, there is no "theory of power," nor even the makings of one. In many respects, this only highlights the fact that Foucault's system is not philosophical but rather epistemological, even though most recent scholarship tends to apply Foucault's descriptions as ontological paradigms rather than as finite genealogical arrangements that can undergo quite sudden historical transformations.

Since Foucault's untimely death in 1984, there have many interpretations of the concept of biopower, and this trend has only intensified recently with the translation of the lectures beginning in 2003. In conclusion, I will highlight two dominant interpretations of the concept of biopower, in particular, that in many ways have reshaped its original application to social phenomena, causing a mutation of its historical specificity, according to the major interpretation offered by French philosopher Gilles Deleuze, and perhaps even the deformation of its positive genealogical sense in favor of a more ontologically inflected reading offered by Italian philosopher Giorgio Agamben. Once again, it is not simply by accident that in 1988 and in 2006, respectively, each attempted to appropriate Foucault's major conceptual device with the same question: "What is a dispositif?"

In the year immediately following Foucault's death, Deleuze, who was a longtime interlocutor and former colleague, conducts his own seminar on Foucault's major concepts, which is published in 1986 and described as "a portrait of the philosopher and his work."[12] However, it is not until the postscript that appears several years later do we find a description of a new biopolitical order of "control" that is emerging to replace disciplinary society.[13] Deleuze explicitly proposes a program to identify the new mechanisms of control in terms of the following problem: how to locate and identify all the elements of a multiplicity in an open or relatively unlimited and "smooth" space. This is contrasted to the social problem of a disciplinary order, much like the one also described by Althusser, which is how to locate a relative number of elements of a finite multiplicity within a closed space (the factory, the school, the prison, the hospital). Thus a spatiotemporal "diagram" is introduced into Foucault's earlier analysis of disciplinary society, supplanting the positive role of concrete dispositifs of Foucault's earlier analysis of sexuality and security. For Deleuze, moreover, the emphasis is no longer placed on the emergence of biopolitics in the nineteenth century but rather on the creation of a program for outlining the potential of future forms of resistance, that is, the shape of the power relations to come, which in the present moment constitute the "outside" of disciplinary enclosures and are composed of purely virtual and unformed power relations and new subjectivities.

To be fair, perhaps what Deleuze is attempting to describe is also what Foucault had addressed in the statement quoted earlier: that the greatest source of new resistance is the submission to the earlier normative and disciplinary forms of subjectivity. In the conclusion of his brief "postscript," Deleuze himself worries whether these new forms of resistance will only lead to a more powerful form of confinement than discipline could ever dream—a confinement fashioned by the continuous process of subjectification through the production of new forms of human capital demanded by late capitalist societies. For example, Deleuze sees this danger in what he observes as the "strange craving" of the youth to be motivated or in the demands for new vocational training and "special courses for continuing education."[14] In response, we might come simply to understand Deleuze's own vision of control society as also historically dated, because it hails from the early introduction of neoliberal policies into French society during the period of the early 1980s (specifically, the break with the dirigiste model in 1983). However, as a purely regional and somewhat parochial point of view on the impact of globalization on one society alone, it cannot be employed paradigmatically as an image of the society to come. A more progressive interpretation will later be found in the work of Hardt and Negri, who, in the trilogy beginning with *Empire* (2000), synthesize Deleuze's and Foucault's theories in the construction of an "affirmative biopolitics" premised on the continuous production and reproduction of new forms of living labor, that is, when the subjectification of life itself is equal to resistance.[15]

Given the identification of resistance with the new forms of living labor, perhaps a more accurate term for what Deleuze called "control society" is simply *enterprise society,* which Foucault himself employs to distinguish between disciplinary and biopolitical techniques of subjectification and their concrete dispositifs. After discussing these techniques in the seminar of February 14, 1979, Foucault concludes, "An enterprise society and a judicial society framed by the multiplicity of juridical institutions, are two faces of a single phenomenon."[16] In other words, here we see a very different relationship between so-called discipline and so-called control that cannot be represented by historical periodicity or succession (e.g., "we are quitting disciplinary society and arriving at something new") but rather something of the multiplication of centers of action, all of which belong to the contemporary moment. For example, today we continue to witness the multiplication of new juridical and normative mechanisms that have emerged to limit—or, at least, to mediate—the growing number of conflicts engendered by capitalist production and reproduction, which Foucault early on described as the multiplication of surfaces of friction and potential legal disputes that emerge between the private and the public (as well as political) spheres. Of course, it also follows that many of these mechanisms expand beyond the threshold of political authority (or national sovereignty) and can no longer be centralized on the state form, as later exemplified in Hardt and Negri's refashioning of the concept of civil society to now exist "outside" of the historical nation-states.

I will now turn to one of the most paradigmatic and influential rein-
terpretations of the concept of biopower, which is the one offered by Giorgio Agamben in his groundbreaking work *Homo Sacer* (1998). As is well
known, in the opening pages of his major argument concerning the inti-
mate relationship between sovereign power and bare life, founded upon
the Greek concepts of *bios* and *zoe*, Agamben stages a direct confrontation
with Foucault's genealogy of biopolitics, from the final chapter of *The History of Sexuality*, "The Right of Death and Power over Life," to the last seminar on the "subject of power" given at the University of Vermont in 1982.
Returning to the question of Foucault's method and what I have identified
as a "axiomatized analysis of power," Agamben explicitly challenges what
he perceives then as the "decisive abandonment of the traditional approach
to power, which is based on juridico-institutional models (the definition of
sovereignty, the theory of the State)," in favor of the study of new political
techniques and technologies of subjectification that are present throughout Foucault's later works and lectures.[17] "Clearly," he writes, "these two
lines [of research] (which carry on two tendencies present in Foucault's
work from the very beginning) intersect in many points and refer back to
a common center."[18] What is this "common center," and what would be the
function of a center in the foregoing description? Since Descartes and Spinoza, the question of philosophical method has been based on the art of
geometry; the function of a center is the virtual point where at least three
lines converge or intersect. However, the diagram of Foucault's method
that Agamben provides is of two lines that may intersect at many points
and may "refer to a common center" but in fact never converge. According to Agamben, this missing center produces "something like a vanishing
point that the different lines of Foucault's inquiry *(and, more generally, of
the entire Western reflection on power)* converge toward without ever reach-
ing."[19] Therefore, he asks, if Foucault's method contests the traditional approach to power, then where do these lines of research intersect?

Of course, it is here that Agamben infamously defines the point of
their intersection as a "blind spot in the eye of the researcher himself."[20]
Immediately following, in perhaps one of the most remarkably counterintuitive statements in the history of contemporary philosophy, Agamben
claims that in fact there is nothing new in Foucault's "reflection on power."[21]
Therefore he completely disregards Foucault's emphasis on the array of dis-

ciplinary knowledges that will compose the new political techniques, "such as the police sciences," which, in the later article on the concept of the dispositif, he will characterize as merely the process of the "secularization" of knowledge-power in modernity that "profanes, in the most problematic manner," what is essentially a theological genealogy of biopolitical apparatuses.[22] In other words, despite all their purported innovations and new technical terms, Foucault's reflections on power only manage to extend the perspectival lines that already belong to "the entire Western reflection on power" a little farther outward toward a distant vanishing point where the "hidden meaning of the political itself gets lost on that same horizon."[23] As a result, the "practical calling of politics" also remains to this day in a state of "concealment" in the very blindness that appears at the very end of this reflection, if not in the eye of Foucault himself. At this point of blindness and insight, Agamben reveals the original, if yet still concealed, "nucleus of sovereign power" that will henceforth function in his own research as the point of intersection between the juridico-institutional and biopolitical models of power.[24]

In response to these claims, let's return now to Foucault's own line of research by recalling the earlier statement from *The History of Sexuality* (immediately following the sections on "method, domain, and periodization") that the "age of biopower" could be said to have commenced when the two lines defined above (i.e., disciplinary techniques and the new knowledges of political economy), which were still separated by the end of the eighteenth century and joined at the level of discourse (e.g., "ideology"), gradually converged in forming the "concrete assemblages" *(agencements concrets)* of the dispositifs of sexuality and security. Moreover, it is at the center of each dispositif that the subject of power itself will emerge as a "complex idea" that can no longer be completely rationalized by the traditional forms of sovereignty or a theory of the state. Certainly, in response, one may ask, Where is sovereignty? or Whither the state? but no longer according to the classical Euclidian coordinates belonging to the previous representation of sovereignty, as if asking, Where is the center? or Where is the nucleus of all power relations? Foucault will return to this point at the beginning of the lecture courses each year, if only to qualify and further refine his method of analysis, and, of course, to defend his decision to "bypass or get around the problem of sovereignty . . . and to reveal the problem of domination and subjugation instead."[25] Thus he immediately adds in the first of a series of "methodological precautions," which function as the postulates of his research, that "our objective is not to analyze rule-governed and legitimate forms of power that have a single center [i.e., sovereignty], or to look at what its general mechanisms or its overall effects might be [i.e., the state, juridico-legal institutions, etc.]."[26]

Does this mean that the question concerning sovereignty in particular disappears entirely from Foucault's reflections or is "decisively abandoned altogether," according to Agamben's major claim? In response to this question, I will conclude my own study simply by making a few counterclaims by pointing out the exact locations where Foucault's three lines actually do intersect again around the question of sovereignty—but following the coordinates of a new convention or conceptual diagram. First, there is Foucault's response to the very same objection at the beginning of the lecture course of 1978—that is, seventeen years before Agamben!—that, in point of fact, "the problem sovereignty is not eliminated by the emergence of a new art of government that has crossed the threshold of the political sciences; on the contrary, it is made more acute than ever before."[27] At this point, Foucault in some ways addresses the problem of periodization I have noted earlier in Deleuze's account of the molting of the diagram itself between disciplinary order and biopolitical control. As Foucault argues,

> the idea of government as a government of population makes the problem of the foundation of sovereignty even more acute (and we have Rousseau) and it makes the need to develop disciplines even more acute (and we have the history of disciplines that I have tried to analyze elsewhere). So, we should not see things as the replacement of the society of sovereignty by the society of discipline, and then of a society of discipline by a society of, say, governmentality. In fact, *we have a triangle*: sovereignty, discipline, and governmental management, which has population as its main target and apparatuses of security as its essential mechanism *(dispositif)*.[28]

However, with this last statement, we still have not located the exact intersection of the aforementioned lines of research but have only arrived at the figure of three separate lines (sovereignty, discipline, governmentality) in the form of a triangle. But, to echo Agamben's earlier question, where do these lines intersect?

In point of fact, the three lines of research intersect in the "milieu." What is a "milieu"? In the conclusion of the lecture of January 11, 1978, Foucault imports this critical term, once again, by citing Canguilhem on the emergence of the idea of milieu, which was imported into biology by mechanics in the second half of the eighteenth century.[29] "The problem to be solved for mechanics in Newton's time," Canguilhem observed, "was that of the action at a distance of distinct physical individuals," for which Foucault will provide the "target" of population as a new object of governmentality.[30] However, what is most striking in the idea of "milieu" that now belongs to the field of biology is that it forms the intersection between the "nature" of the natural sciences and the "nature of the human species" from that point onward. As Canguilhem first observes, "after three centuries of experimental and mathematical physics, *milieu,* which in physics signified *environment,* has come to signify *center*—in both physics and biology."[31] Nevertheless, as Foucault cautions,

> to say that this is the sudden emergence of the "naturalness" of the human species in the field of the techniques of power would be excessive [even though he concludes that it is something fundamental to what he calls "biopower"]. But what [before] then appeared above all in the form of need, insufficiency, or weakness, illness, now appears at the intersection between a multiplicity of living individuals working and coexisting with each other in a set of material elements that act on them and on which they act in turn.[32]

In short, the "milieu" is now the primary *target* for the intervention of power. In other words, here we bear witness to the appearance of a fourth "element" of Foucault's biopolitical dispositif—if not the notion of the "milieu" itself, then at least the "appearance of a project, a political technique that will be aimed at the milieu."[33] It is at this "intersection" between physical material nature and the nature of the species that we might now ask, Where is sovereignty? As Foucault responds, the sovereign is precisely the permanent conjunction between these two different natures, a form of sovereignty that from this point is very different from the judicial notion of sovereignty and territory, and from disciplinary space as well, *since its goal is nothing less than to transform the "naturalness" (natura naturans) of the two natures.* As Foucault concludes (and thus as I will conclude my study of the analytic of biopower as well):

> you can see that we again encounter the problem of the sovereign here, but the sovereign is no longer someone who exercises power over a territory on the basis of a geographical localization of his political sovereignty. The sovereign deals with a nature, or rather the perpetual conjunction, the perpetual imbrication of geographical, climactic, and physical milieu with the human species insofar as it has a body and a soul, a physical and a moral existence; and the sovereign will have to be someone who will have to exercise power at the point of connection where nature, in the sense of physical elements, interferes with the nature of the human species, at that point of articulation where the milieu itself becomes the determining factor. *This is where the sovereign will have to intervene, if he wants to change the human species.*[34]

Acknowledgments

This study of Foucault's analytic of biopower was conceived and written as a final report for the Society for the Study of Bio-political Futures, a five-year research initiative convened in spring 2013 in the Humanities Center at Syracuse University and disbanded in fall 2018 at the annual meeting of the SLSA in Toronto. This is not intended as a collective statement, because the society was defined from the very beginning as a finite community of researchers who came for an equally finite period of time "to construct the collective analysis of the concept of biopower that is dispersed throughout our own individual research and writing projects." A website has been created to archive this group's research objectives, membership, and international meetings and is located at http:// biopoliticalfutures.net/. I wish to thank all those who participated in this unique research group, especially my closest friends and colleagues, Jeffrey T. Nealon, Paul Patton, and Cary Wolfe. As always, I wish to thank my editor, Douglas Armato, for his steadfast support and perseverance with such an incorrigible author-function. Finally, some portions of this study have previously appeared in translation or in the following journals and critical editions: "Le dispositif généologie du concept" (translated in French), *Cahiers de L'Agart,* January 2019; "Notes toward an Investigation of Control Society," in *Cultures of Control,* edited by Frida Beckman (Edinburgh: Edinburgh University Press, 2018); "Biopolitics and Biopower," in *Bloomsbury Handbook of Literary and Cultural Theory,* edited by Jeffrey R. Di Leo (London: Bloomsbury, 2017). I wish to acknowledge and thank the editors of these publications, Frida Beckman, Jeffrey R. Di Leo, and Philip Armstrong.

Notes

ARTICLE I. ON "FOUCAULT"

1. Foucault, *Archeology of Knowledge,* 215.

2. Foucault, 221.

3. The following extends my reflections on the "art of commentary" in *Non-philosophy of Gilles Deleuze*; see the preface, ix–xiv.

4. Foucault, *Archeology of Knowledge,* 221.

5. I have addressed elsewhere the difference between the "author-function" and the more dynamic role of what I call the "conceptual persona," following Deleuze and Guattari in "Who Are Deleuze and Guattari's Conceptual Personae?" See also Lambert, "Joy of Surfing with Deleuze and Guattari."

6. Foucault, *Archeology of Knowledge,* 224.

7. Foucault, 222.

8. Foucault, 228, my emphasis.

9. Foucault, 224.

10. Foucault, "The Human Sciences," in *Order of Things,* 375–421.

11. Foucault, *Archeology of Knowledge,* 223.

12. My archeological legend is primarily based on the translation history of his works, and especially on the discursive effect produced by the translation of the lectures between 2003 and 2008. Of course, different arrangements or discursive groupings are indeed possible, and some readers might even want to include a fifth age concerning the "Care of Self" (see Nealon, *Foucault beyond Foucault,* 1–6). Nevertheless, despite any genealogical imprecision, I have chosen the four ages of "Foucault" (and the corresponding four "anti-Foucaults") in analogy to the four elements, the four seasons, the four metals or ages of industry, the four levels of interpretation in Aquinas, and so on. To add a fifth age would violate the rule of symmetry that I employ throughout my study of the current age of "Foucault."

13. Elden, *Foucault: The Last Decade*, 2. As Elden further recounts in his excellent archival study, "in the letter written eighteen months before his death, which in the absence of a formal document has been legally interpreted as his will, Foucault made his views on this subject clear: 'No posthumous publications' (*DE*, vol. 4, 13–64)."

14. Foucault, "What Is an Author?," in *Language, Counter-memory, Practice*, 117.

15. Foucault, *Archeology of Knowledge*, 221.

16. Foucault, "What Is an Author?," 138.

17. Nealon, *Foucault beyond Foucault*, 5.

18. Nealon.

19. Deleuze, *Foucault*, 96.

20. Once again, Stuart Elden's very insightful bibliographic and archival research has revealed a much more complicated history of the departure from the original plan for six volumes of *The History of Sexuality*. Instead of a long period of silence, whether understood heroically, as failure, or as a symptom of psychological malaise, a different story tells of an argument with the editor of Gallimard, Pierre Nora, in 1980 over Foucault's perceived lack of support for François Mitterrand. According to Elden, Foucault even threatened to leave Gallimard and to publish the remaining volumes of his history of sexuality elsewhere. Elden, *Last Foucault*, 2.

21. Kafka, *"Metamorphosis,"* 137.

22. Foucault, *Archeology of Knowledge*, 218.

23. Foucault, 224.

24. Foucault, *Dit et écrits*, 4:571.

25. On the function of what I am calling "global polemics," see the conclusion of my *Return Statements*.

26. Foucault, *Security, Territory, Population*, 3–4.

27. Foucault, *History of Sexuality*, 1:159.

28. See Canguilhem, *Knowledge of Life*, 70.

29. "Postulates" *(postulata)* are traditionally understood as unproven axioms proposed at the beginning of a synthetic demonstration as a series of hypotheses, but rhetorically, they should be understood as a series of "requests to the reader or audience," which was the dominant sense of Descartes's use of the term in *Objections*. Foucault was clearly aware of this earlier sense, and thus each of the lecture years commences by proposing a series of "requests," "hypotheses," or *"un certain nombre de propositions, propositions au sens d'indications de choix; ce ne sont ni des principes, ni des règles, ni de théorèmes."* Foucault, *Security, Territory, Population*, 3ff.

30. Descartes, *Objections*, 34–35.

1. METHOD

1. Euclid, *Elements*, 1:3.

2. From this point onward, I will naturalize my use of the French term *dispositif* for the purpose of technical accuracy and in keeping with its precise meaning in the fields of biology, following Canguilhem, and geometry, where Foucault first derives the concept from the Cartesian *more geometrico dispositae,* which refers to a synthetic and artificial order of demonstration that is reserved for certain questions (see Descartes, *Objections,* 34–41). For the sake of consistency with the terms variously employed in the English translations, and in certain specific contexts, I will also use the terms *conceptual device, diagram, mechanism, machine,* and *apparatus.*

3. Leibniz, *New Essays,* IV, II, 13.

4. Descartes, *Objections,* 35.

5. Foucault, *History of Sexuality,* 1:93. The notion of deformation should not immediately be taken negatively, as in criticism or hermeneutics of interpretation, but rather as a principle of vitality in the life of the concept, such as in the regions of linguistic morphology and evolutionary biology.

6. Canguilhem, *Knowledge of Life,* 92.

7. Canguilhem, 93.

8. Canguilhem.

9. Canguilhem.

10. Foucault, *Order of Things,* 407–20.

11. Years 1978–79, Naissance de la biopolitique; 1979–80, Du gouvernement des vivants; 1980–81, Subjectivité et Vérité; 1981–82, L'Herméneutique du sujet; 1982–83, Le Gouvernement de soi et des autres; 1983–84, Le courage de la vérité.

12. Foucault, *Security, Territory, Population,* 3.

13. Foucault.

14. Foucault, *Dits et écrits,* 3:541.

15. Foucault, 3:541–42.

16. Descartes, *Objections,* 37.

17. Qtd. in Blanché, *Axiomatics,* 7.

18. Blanché.

19. Blanché, 8.

20. Foucault, *Histoire de la sexualité,* 1:201.

21. Foucault, *Security, Territory, Population,* 1.

22. Ibid.

23. Blanché, *Axiomatics,* 3.

24. See Deleuze, "On Kant."

25. Goldenbaum, "Geometric Method."

26. Foucault, *Dits et écrits,* 3:542.

27. Foucault, *History of Sexuality,* 1:92–93.

28. Foucault, 1:93.

29. Foucault.

30. Foucault.

31. Foucault, 1:97.

32. Foucault, 1:92. I constantly highlight the mistranslation of Foucault's own text, in which the translator often substitutes literal geometric terms for Foucault's own language ("sphere" for *"domaine,"* "circle" for *"champs"*). Nevertheless, this only furthers my argument that the metaphorical equivalence of the geometrical figures simply expresses the "common notions" that belong to the traditional representations of power. As I argue throughout this study, these are merely the figurative terms that compose our most common and habitual mental pictures of power, which allows us to orient ourselves in the field composed of power relations, both real and imaginary.

33. Foucault, *Language, Counter-memory, Practices,* 214

34. Kafka, "Metamorphosis," 148.

35. Foucault, *History of Sexuality,* 1:93.

36. Foucault, *Discipline and Punish,* 202.

2. CONCEPTUAL DEVICE

1. Foucault, *Archeology of Knowledge,* 86.

2. Agamben, *What Is an Apparatus?,* 5.

3. Deleuze, *Two Regimes of Madness,* 338–41.

4. Bryukhovetska, "'Dispositif' Theory."

5. On this point, I am in agreement with Matteo Pasquinelli's recent criticism of Agamben's etymological method to trace modern "secularized" juridical concepts to their supposed theological sources (which, interestingly enough, bears more than a passing resemblance to Heidegger's etymology of Greek concepts), when he writes, "The history of the idea of the dispositif in Foucault is, of course, plural and complex, but it can be more easily explained without the detour through an archaic Christian government of *oikonomia.*" See Pasquinelli, "What an Apparatus Is *Not,*" 80ff.

6. Deleuze, *Two Regimes of Madness,* 338.

7. Deleuze.

8. Deleuze, *Foucault,* 27.

9. See esp. Althusser, "Pourquoi donc L'État est-il une machine?," in *Écrits,* 1:449–54.

10. See *Micro Robert: Dictionnaire du francais primordial*, s.v. "appareil."

11. Althusser, *Écrits*, 1:449–50.

12. Foucault, *Discipline and Punish*, 169.

13. Foucault, my emphasis.

14. Of course, I am referring to the celebrated article "Ideologie et appareils ideologique d'État," which first appeared in 1970 and, then again, in a reprised version in 1976 in *Positions*.

15. Foucault, *Abnormal*, 49.

16. Foucault, *Power/Knowledge*, 196.

17. Foucault, 52.

18. Canguilhem, *Oeuvres complètes*, 4:647–48.

19. Foucault, *History of Sexuality*, 1:93.

20. Foucault, *Abnormal*, 52.

21. Agamben, *What Is an Apparatus?*, 8. On this point, see again Pasquinelli, "What an Apparatus Is *Not*," 79.

22. Foucault, *Security, Territory, Population*, 8.

23. Foucault, *Power/Knowledge*, 196.

24. Foucault, *History of Sexuality*, 1:104–5.

25. Foucault, 1:154–55.

26. Foucault, 1:155.

27. Foucault, *Histoire de la sexualité*, 1:201.

28. Foucault, *History of Sexuality*, 1:155.

29. Foucault, 1:159.

30. Foucault, *Ethics*, 228.

31. Foucault, *Abnormal*, 50.

32. Foucault.

33. Althusser, *"Lenin and Philosophy" and Other Essays*, 113.

34. Althusser, 96n8.

35. Althusser, 107.

36. Althusser, 119.

37. Althusser, 116.

38. Deleuze, "On Kant."

39. Deleuze (translation modified).

40. Althusser, Lenin and Philosophy, 107.

41. Althusser.

42. Althusser, 115.

43. Althusser.

44. Canguilhem, *Knowledge of Life*, 83.

45. Foucault, *Security, Territory, Population*, 10.

46. Canguilhem, *Oeuvres complètes*, 4:625–42.

47. Canguilhem, *Knowledge of Life*, 76.

48. Canguilhem, 83.

49. Canguilhem.

50. Canguilhem, 81ff.

51. Althusser, *Écrits*, 1:452.

52. Althusser, 1:453.

53. Canguilhem, *Knowledge of Life*, 86.

54. Canguilhem.

55. Canguilhem, 83.

56. Foucault, *Abnormal*, 51.

57. Foucault, *Security, Territory, Population*, 6.

3. GRID OF INTELLIGIBILITY

1. Foucault, *Security, Territory, Population*, 48.

2. See also chapter 2 of Dillon, *Biopolitics of Security*, 45–75.

3. Pasquinelli, "What an Apparatus Is *Not*," 82.

4. Pasquinelli.

5. Foucault, *Birth of Biopolitics*, 80ff.

6. Foucault, 185ff. Also see pp. 218ff for a brief comparison of the different national forms of neoliberalism up to this period.

7. Foucault, *Security, Territory, Population*, 107. Concerning the inclusion of animals and other species in the problem of the government of the living, see Wolfe, *Before the Law*.

8. Qtd. in Foucault, *Birth of Biopolitics*, 157.

9. Foucault, 243.

10. Foucault, 270.

11. Foucault, 148.

12. Prittie, *Life World Library*, 71–72.

13. Foucault, *Birth of Biopolitics*, 150.

14. Foucault, *Security, Territory, Population*, 109.

15. Foucault, *Birth of Biopolitics*, 241.

16. Foucault.

17. The other sources that Foucault heavily relies upon are more contemporary, including official proceedings and reports from the French Ministry of Economy and Finance and personal confidences with the technical advisor to the cabinet of V. Giscard d'Estaing, Lionel Stoléru, who was also secretary for the Ministry of Labor in 1978 and the author of *Vaincre le pauvreté* (1977). (Foucault cites

these personal exchanges with Stoléru extensively in the lecture of March 7, 1979.) Here I am also underscoring the fact that most of Foucault's sources were very contemporary and, indeed, very "Parisian," that is, belonging to a young elite class of French technical bureaucrats. Consequently, most of his knowledge of neoliberalism was filtered through the French intelligentsia of his own time.

18. Foucault, 185.

19. Foucault, 295.

20. Foucault, 283.

21. Foucault, 150.

22. Foucault, 297.

23. Hayek, qtd. in Mirowski and Plehwe, *Road from Mont Pèlerin,* 443.

24. Foucault, *Birth of Biopolitics,* 302.

25. Foucault, *Abnormal,* 51.

26. Ordoliberalism first emerges in the prewar period from the members of the Freiburg School (Euken, Bohm, Röpke, Rüstow) and comes from the term *Ordnungspolitik,* or "policy of order" *(Ordo),* which later evolved into a *Gesellschaftspolitik* commonly associated with the postwar "social market theory" in the GDR. It is significant to note that Foucault's account of the history of postwar neoliberalism through the mid-1970s places greater emphasis on this school of thought than on Hayek and the Chicago School—although he was speaking prior to the schism that occurred between Hayek and Friedman in the early 1980s.

27. Rüstow, *Freedom and Domination,* 468.

28. Rüstow, 438.

29. Mirowski and Plehwe, *Road from Mont Pèlerin,* 445.

30. Mirowski and Plehwe, 443.

31. Rüstow, *Freedom and Domination,* 469.

32. Foucault, *Birth of Biopolitics,* 297.

33. Foucault, 298.

34. Foucault, 309.

35. Rüstow, *Freedom and Domination,* 659.

36. Rüstow, 459.

37. Deleuze, *Pourparlers,* 246.

38. Deleuze, 246–47.

39. In fact, *Cinema 1: L'Image mouvement* appears in 1983, *Cinema 2: L'Imagetemps* in 1985, the same year as Deleuze's seminar on Foucault, which I will refer to later.

40. Deleuze and Guattari, *A Thousand Plateaus,* 485ff.

41. Deleuze and Guattari, 485.

42. Deleuze and Guattari.

43. Deleuze, *Pourparlers,* 246.

44. Deleuze and Guattari, *A Thousand Plateaus,* 570n57.

45. Neil Gaiman's introduction to Bradbury, *Fahrenheit 451,* 30–31.

46. Deleuze and Guattari, *A Thousand Plateaus,* 459.

47. Maurice Blanchot, qtd. in Deleuze, *Foucault,* 43.

48. Deleuze, *Foucault,* 13.

49. Dean and Villadsen, *State Phobia,* 110.

50. See also Kelly's cogent criticism in "Discipline Is Control."

51. Deleuze, *Foucault,* 86.

52. Deleuze, *Pourparlers,* 247.

53. As an example of this excessive formalization of Foucault's diagrams, allow me to quote from the original script of the 1986 seminar: "[J]e dirais: le diagramme vient du dehors, mais on ne sait pas ce que Foucault peut bien entendre par « dehors ». Seconde réponse : le diagramme vient toujours d'un autre diagramme. Ah ouais ; pourquoi ? Parce que tout diagramme est mutation. Tout diagramme est mutation d'un diagramme précédent qui était déjà mutation. Le diagramme est fondamentalement mutant. Il exprime même, dans une société, les mutations possibles. Bien. Comment réunir les deux . . . à entrer en mutation. Il va de soi que si le diagramme n'était pas parsemé de points de résistance, il n'y aurait pas de mutations. C'est les points de résistance qui forcent et qui entraînent une mutation du diagramme, c'est-à-dire un second tirage qui vient du dehors, non moins que le précédent, qui aura aussi ses points de résistance, et un troisième tirage etc. qui a eu euh . . . , donc, déterminer . . . pas déterminer, qui va enclencher les mutations. C'est lorsque les points de résistance se globalisent qu'à ce moment-là il va y avoir renversement du diagramme au profit d'un nouveau diagramme. Si bien que . . . qu'est-ce que. . . . A la limite je pourrais dire : on en a fini maintenant. Parce que qu'est-ce que c'est que cette résistance, d'où ça vient, tout ça ? Il faudra essayer de le voir, mais, en gros, on a fini avec l'axe du pouvoir. Puisqu'on a déjà dépassé le pouvoir . . . : ah, écoute, je ne crois pas que ce soit la même chose, je ne sais pas, tu me diras ce que tu veux dire. Est-ce qu'il faut, là, dire . . . ? Pour le moment, là, nous on en est là. C'est au-delà des diagrammes il y a encore autre chose qui est cette ligne du dehors dont les diagrammes sortent, dont les diagrammes sont issus ; c'est la ligne qui lance les dés, si j'ose dire, c'est la ligne qui lance les dés, alors, en ce sens, ce serait la ligne de Nietzsche, on pourrait, on pourrait en faire comme des nœuds sur cette ligne : Melville, Michaux, Nietzsche, Proust si vous voulez, tout ça . . . et, bon, alors, bien, peut-être qu'on a été trop vite." Gilles Deleuze/Foucault, Le Pouvoir course 13, February 25, 1986.

54. See esp. Foucault's late article on Canguilhem, "La vie: l'experience et la science," *Dits et écrits,* 2:1582–95.

55. Deleuze, *Foucault*, 90.

56. For example, this underlies Wendy Brown's recent treatment of neoliberalism as well as her accusation of Foucault's decisive abandonment of the Marxist framework of the "State-Form" as seemingly the only corrective to the universality of market power: "Foucault's seemingly light judgments against neoliberalism pertain not only to his admirable commitment to excavating the novelties that only a genealogical curiosity can discover. . . . Rather, Foucault *averted his glance* from capital itself as a historical and social force." (I have emphasized the phrase "averted his glance," which I will return to discussing in article III vis-à-vis Agamben's influential trope.) See Brown, *Undoing the Demos*, 74–75.

57. Foucault, *Birth of Biopolitics*, 76.

58. Jameson, *Political Unconscious*, 54n.

59. Jameson.

60. Jameson.

61. See Wolfe's pragmatic treatment of the function of "political utopias" in the criticism of Foucault's genealogy of biopolitics, which draws as much from Niklas Luhmann as from Foucault concerning the absence of the state as a steering mechanism of the political system, in "Posthumanism Thinks the Political," 130ff.

62. Deleuze and Guattari, *A Thousand Plateaus*, 427.

63. Foucault, *Birth of Biopolitics*, 77.

64. Foucault.

65. Foucault, 130.

66. Foucault.

67. Deleuze and Guattari, *A Thousand Plateaus*, 472. They employ the paradigm of the "mega-machine," in a strict sense, according to Mumford's first use of the term in *Myth of the Machine*, 12: "Conceptually the instruments of mechanization five thousand years ago were already detached from other human functions and purposes than the constant increase of order, power, predictability, and, above all, control. With this proto-scientific ideology went a corresponding regimentation and degradation of once-autonomous human activities: 'mass culture' and 'mass control' made their first appearance." For another description of the "machinic form of enslavement," based on the same passage from *A Thousand Plateaus*, see Lazzarato, *Signs and Machines*, 43–52.

68. Foucault, *Birth of Biopolitics*, 187.

69. Deleuze and Guattari, *A Thousand Plateaus*, 495ff.

70. Hardt and Negri, *Commonwealth*, 59.

71. Deleuze and Guattari, *A Thousand Plateaus*, 570.

72. Foucault, *Birth of Biopolitics*, 189.

73. Foucault, 188.

74. Foucault, 76.

75. The final list of statements, which could be called "critical commonplaces of contemporary critical theory," is compiled from the writings of Deleuze and Guattari, Agamben, Lazzaretto, and Virilio.

76. Kafka, *Castle*, 3.

77. Foucault, *Birth of Biopolitics*, 77.

78. Foucault.

79. Foucault, 67.

80. Mirowski and Plehwe, *Road from Mont Pèlerin*, 437ff.

81. Deleuze and Guattari, *A Thousand Plateaus*, 570.

ARTICLE III. ON THE MUTATIONS OF BIOPOWER

1. Descartes, *Objections*, 35–36.

2. Foucault, *History of Sexuality*, 1:152.

3. Foucault, *"Society Must Be Defended,"* 14.

4. Foucault, *Birth of Biopolitics*, 271.

5. Foucault, *Abnormal*, 25.

6. Foucault, *"Society Must Be Defended,"* 245.

7. Foucault.

8. Foucault, *Abnormal*, 53.

9. Pasquinelli, "What an Apparatus Is *Not*," 82.

10. Foucault, *History of Sexuality*, 1:140.

11. Foucault, *Power and Subjectivity*, 228.

12. Deleuze, *Foucault*; see also Deleuze, "A Portrait of Foucault," in *Negotiations*, 102–18.

13. Deleuze's "Postscript on the Societies of Control" first appears in *L'Autre Journal*, no. 1 (May 1990).

14. Deleuze, *Pourparlers*, 247. For the best description of this new form of confinement, the intensification of confinement by the form of subjectification itself, see Nealon's account in *Foucault beyond Foucault*, 94–112.

15. Hardt and Negri, *Commonwealth*, 59.

16. Foucault, *Birth of Biopolitics*, 150.

17. Agamben, *Homo Sacer*, 5.

18. Agamben.

19. Agamben, 6.

20. Agamben.

21. Agamben.

22. Agamben, *What Is a Dispositif?*, 19.

23. Agamben.

24. Agamben, *Homo Sacer,* 6.

25. Foucault, *"Society Must Be Defended,"* 27.

26. Foucault.

27. Foucault, *Security, Territory, Population,* 107.

28. Foucault, 107–8, my emphasis.

29. Foucault, 36n. See also Canguilhem, *Knowledge of Life,* 102ff.

30. Canguilhem, *Knowledge of Life.*

31. Canguilhem, 70.

32. Foucault, *Security, Territory, Population,* 37n.

33. Foucault, 38.

34. Foucault, my emphasis.

Bibliography

Agamben, Giorgio. *Homo Sacer: Sovereign Power and Bare Life*. Palo Alto, Calif.: Stanford University Press, 1995.

Agamben, Giorgio. *What Is an Apparatus?* Palo Alto, Calif.: Stanford University Press, 2009.

Althusser, Louis. *Écrits philosophiques et politiques*. Book 1. Paris: Stock, 1994.

Althusser, Louis. *"Lenin and Philosophy" and Other Essays*. New York: Monthly Review Press, 2001.

Althusser, Louis. *Positions*. Paris: Editions Sociales, 1976.

Anonymous. "Matter." In *The Catholic World: General Science and Literature,* vol. 20, *1874–1875*. New York: Catholic Publication House.

Blanché, Robert. *Axiomatics*. London: Routledge, 1962.

Bradbury, Ray. *Fahrenheit 451*. New York: Simon and Schuster, 2012.

Brown, Wendy. *Undoing the Demos: Neoliberalism's Stealth Revolution*. New York: Zone Books, 2015.

Bryukhovetska, Olga. "'Dispositif' Theory: Returning to the Movie Theater." http://www.art-it.asia/.

Canguilhem, Georges. *Knowledge of Life*. Translated by Stefanos Geroulanos and Daniela Ginsburg. New York: Fordham University Press, 2008.

Canguilhem, Georges. *Oeuvres complètes,* book 4, *Resistance, philosophie, biologique et histoire des sciences 1940–1965*. Paris: Vrin, 2015.

Dean, Mitchell, and Kaspar Villadsen. *State Phobia and Civil Society: Michel Foucault's Political Legacy*. Pala Alto, Calif.: Stanford University Press, 2015.

Deleuze, Gilles. *Foucault*. Translated by Sean Hand. London: Athlone Press, 1988.

Deleuze, Gilles. *Negotiations: 1972–1990*. Translated by Martin Joughin. New York: Columbia University Press.

Deleuze, Gilles. "On Kant." http://deleuzelectures.blogspot.com/2007/02/on -kant.html.

Deleuze, Gilles. *Pourparlers*. Paris: Minuit, 1990.

Deleuze, Gilles. *Two Regimes of Madness: Texts and Interviews 1975–1995*. Edited by David Lapoujade. Translated by Ames Hodges and Mike Taormina. New York: Semiotext(e), 2006.

Deleuze, Gilles, and Félix Guattari. *A Thousand Plateaus*. Translated by Brian Massumi. Minneapolis: University of Minnesota Press, 1987.

Descartes, René. *Objections to the Meditations and Descartes's Replies*. Translated by Jonathan Bennett. http://earlymoderntexts.com/authors/descartes.

Dillon, Michael. *Biopolitics of Security: A Political Analytic of Finitude*. New York: Routledge.

Elden, Stuart. *Foucault: The Last Decade*. London: Polity Press, 2016.

Euclid. *The First Six Books of the Elements of Euclid*. Translated by Oliver Byrne. London: William Pickering, 1847.

Foucault, Michel. *Abnormal: Lectures at the Collège de France 1974–1975*. London: Palgrave, 2003.

Foucault, Michel. *The Archaeology of Knowledge*. Translated by A. M. Sheridan Smith. London: Pantheon Books, 1972.

Foucault, Michel. *The Birth of Biopolitics: Lectures at the Collège de France 1978–1979*. London: Palgrave, 2008.

Foucault, Michel. *Discipline and Punish: The Birth of the Prison*. Translated by Alan Sheridan. New York: Vintage Books, 1977.

Foucault, Michel. *Dits et écrits 1954–1988*. 4 vols. Edited by Daniel Defert and François Ewald. Paris: Gallimard, 1994.

Foucault, Michel. *Ethics: Subjectivity and Truth*. Vol 1. Edited by Paul Rabinow. New York: New Press.

Foucault, Michel. *The History of Sexuality*, vol. 1, *The Will to Knowledge*. London: Penguin, 1978; *Histoire de la sexualité I: La volunté de savoir*. Paris: Gallimard, 1976.

Foucault, Michel. *Language, Counter-memory, Practice: Selected Essays and Interviews*. Edited by Donald Bouchard. Translated by Donald Bouchard and Sherry Simon. Ithaca, N.Y.: Cornell University Press, 1977.

Foucault, Michel. *The Order of Things*. London: Tavistock/Routledge, 1970.

Foucault, Michel. *Power/Knowledge: Selected Interviews and Other Writings, 1972–1977*. Edited by Colin Gordon. New York: Pantheon Books, 1980.

Foucault, Michel. *Security, Territory, Population: Lectures at the Collège de France 1977–1978*. London: Palgrave, 2008.

Foucault, Michel. *"Society Must Be Defended": Lectures at the Collège de France 1975–1976.* London: Palgrave, 2003.

Goldenbaum, Ursula. "The Geometric Method." *Internet Encyclopedia of Philosophy.* https://www.iep.utm.edu/geo-meth/.

Hardt, Michael, and Antonio Negri. *Commonwealth.* Cambridge, Mass.: Harvard University Press, 2009.

Hobbes, Thomas. *"Leviathan," with Selected Variants from the Latin Edition of 1668.* Edited by Edwin Curley. Indianapolis, Ind.: Hackett, 1994.

Jameson, Fredric. *The Political Unconscious: Narrative as a Socially Symbolic Act.* Ithaca, N.Y.: Cornell University Press, 1981.

Kafka, Franz. *The Castle.* New York: Knopf, 1930.

Kafka, Franz. *"The Metamorphosis," "The Penal Colony," and Other Stories.* New York: Schocken Books, 1946.

Kelly, Mark. "Discipline Is Control: Foucault Contra Deleuze." *New Formations* 84/85, no. 1 (2015).

Lambert, Gregg. "The Joy of Surfing with Deleuze and Guattari." *Deleuze and Guattari Studies* 13, no. 1 (2019): 128–35.

Lambert, Gregg. *The Non-philosophy of Gilles Deleuze.* London: Continuum, 2002.

Lambert, Gregg. *Return Statements: The Return of Religion in Contemporary Philosophy.* Edinburgh: Edinburgh University Press, 2017.

Lambert, Gregg. "Who Are Deleuze and Guattari's Conceptual Personae?" In *The Refrains of Freedom,* edited by Dorothea Olkowski and Eftichis Pirovolakis (Bloomington: Indiana University Press, 2019).

Lazzarato, Maurizio. *Signs and Machines: Capitalism and the Production of Subjectivity.* Cambridge, Mass.: MIT Press, 2017.

Leibniz, Gottfried Wilhelm. *New Essays on Human Understanding.* Translated and edited by Peter Remnant and Jonathan Bennett. New York: Cambridge University Press, 1996.

Mirowski, Philip, and Dieter Plehwe. *The Road from Mont Pèlerin: The Making of a Neoliberal Thought Collective.* Cambridge, Mass.: Harvard University Press, 2009.

Mumford, Lewis. *The Myth of the Machine: The Technics of Human Development.* New York: Harcourt, 1967.

Nealon, Jeffrey. *Foucault beyond Foucault: Power and Its Intensifications since 1984.* Palo Alto, Calif.: Stanford University Press, 2008.

Pasquinelli, Matteo. "What an Apparatus Is *Not*: On the Archeology of the Norm in Foucault, Canguilhem, and Goldstein." *Parrhesia,* no. 22 (2015): 79–89.

Prittie, Terence, ed. *Life World Library: Germany.* 1963.

Rüstow, Alexandre von. *Freedom and Domination: A Historical Critique of Civiliza-tion.* Princeton, N.J.: Princeton University Press, 1980.

Wolfe, Cary. *Before the Law: Humans and Other Animals in a Biopolitical Frame.* Chicago: University of Chicago Press, 2012.

Wolfe, Cary. "Posthumanism Thinks the Political: A Genealogy for Foucault's *Birth of Biopolitics.*" *Journal of Posthuman Studies* 1, no. 2 (2017): 117–35.

Index

GREGG LAMBERT is Dean's Professor of Humanities at Syracuse University, New York, and Distinguished International Scholar, Kyung Hee University, South Korea. His previous books with the University of Minnesota Press include *In Search of a New Image of Thought: Gilles Deleuze and the Philosophical Expressionism* and *Philosophy after Friendship: Deleuze's Conceptual Personae*.